LANDLADY

in

PARADISE

~ How Not To ~

W. M. RAEBECK

*In fond and lasting memory of
Homer Doughty,
kind and always willing.*

*Born with a hammer in his hand
(according to his mother).*

ACKNOWLEDGEMENTS

Thank you to Suzy Frank, Suzy Tunney, and
Lorren Van Fossen
for opening the doors.

Lasting gratitude to Homer, Dave, Johnny, and Rosie
for seeing me through.

And special thanks to my tireless helper and friend,
Lila Mortell,
the most positive person I've ever met.

And none of this could've happened without
the Home Depot,
with its one-stop concept for helping homeowners
and its dedicated customer service.

Finally, sincere thanks to Eve Solomon
for feedback and proofreading at just the right moment.

If you like reading that raises your morale and makes you a better person, this isn't it. But if you like stubborn ambition, calculated risks, and laughable stupidity, this could work. And who knows, maybe you *appreciate* the idea of being out of one's league. Puts meat on the bones.

I personally am not innately landlady material, just don't have the DNA. In fact, I probably have all the wrong personality traits for it. That's why, in reading this book, you may repeatedly ask yourself, "Who would DO what she did?" But just know that your own landlord journey will unfold in its own fashion; no one's path or plan matches another's. And take what you can from my tale, because there's useful insight here.

Despite all logistical preparations, though, becoming a landlord can be a bumpy career path. So everyone must pre-assess their risk tolerance, support levels, and strengths …versus what can and might derail them. Even in Paradise!

At the book's beginning, I explain my choice to jump in way over my head, and how, due mainly to my naiveté, things were tougher than expected. Funky things can happen when you go out on a limb, and "going big" can get so uncomfortable it feels like a mistake….

But not everyone's a) as desperate, or even as determined, as I was to ring in financial security for their old age, or b) such a sucker for novelty and adventure.

But your mind may already be made up, like mine was. Hopefully, you're at least smart enough to research things beforehand, like I wasn't—in which case, you might do what I did, only better: fly alone to Paradise (where you know maybe one person, maybe no person), buy a property, and wing it!

Regardless of naiveté or circumstance, strenuous life chapters can still evolve into major blessings. I somehow survived the parade of characters who tango-ed through my rooms, leaving their stories behind, and *did* come out the other side. Despite all my mistakes and whether I'd do it again, my landlady chapter "made" me financially. And I learned about responsibility, commitment, long-term plans, human nature, construction and tools, the local color of Hawai'i, going by the book, and how court cases work.

Seasoned landlords are definitely grown ups.

WARNING

I want to include a warning that I did not heed.

Before I left LA for Kaua'i, with landlording central to my plan, my friend's husband, Robert, who'd previously lived in Hawai'i, tried to alert me about remote island reality—how the isolated locale attracts not just adventurers, but rough riders, even those running from the law. Robert spelled this out, even repeating himself about four times, to the point where his poor wife was begging him to shut up. "But I want her to hear me," he held his ground. "It's a different reality over there. I want to make sure she understands what she's getting into."

People with stars in their eyes or commitment to an agenda rarely register warnings, though. Poised for take off and already owning property in the islands, I wasn't about to abandon the mission. But Robert's words proved true, and now it's me issuing warnings.

1. If your landlord objective is mainly the financial promise, in which case the location (i.e. Paradise) is secondary, you could spare yourself woe by buying property somewhere that attracts responsible, working, family-oriented or health-oriented renters, rather than outliers, diehards, and those with rap sheets.

2. *Nobody has to be a landlord!* Even if you believe you absolutely must (like I did), you needn't do it hundreds or thousands of miles off shore. Yes, that tropical backdrop is everybody's fantasy and landlording's one way to buy in, but it's not the only nor most fun way to live in Paradise. If you

haven't yet purchased a rental property, ruminate on how far you'll be from your parents, how soon they'll be old, and how far you'll be from your grandchildren and how soon they'll be older.

3. Whatever type of person you are is likely the type of landlord you'll be—hands-on or hands-off; farming out all the chores versus performing them yourself; lax with tenants versus strict; fastidious about maintaining the property versus unconcerned; suspicious of all humankind versus believing everyone is inherently good.

But I'm not here to snuff dreams, so don't let me scare ya! But, as my mother used to say, "For God's sake, make your own mistakes, don't make mine!"

My wish for you—whatever phase or pre-phase of landlording you're in or contemplating—is that after reading this, should you proceed with the quest, you'll be spared drama and despair. And where I commenced landlording naive, green, and out of place, you, my friend, will soon have a Ph. D in the subject.

~ WMR

NOTES

- 'Landlady in Paradise' details numerous landlord issues, many pertaining to a remote locale. Throughout the book, you'll see important points designated as "*LESSONS.*" These aren't assignments for the reader, but rather *lessons learned* by the author. And all are reprinted at the end of the book for review or reference.

- This content will be most useful for would-be landlords and landladies without know-how and/or support—not just women, but anyone lacking construction skills or a strong counterpart. But aside from naturals who sleep in their tool belts, or couples from Idaho (born for this stuff), there are many out there who can also benefit from this material.

- Aside from the "lessons," there are loads of pointers, tips, and advice here. So if this subject matter is new to you, using a highlighter to mark some of the instruction might help you refer back later on.

- This account took place before on-line shopping was the go-to means for procuring goods and materials. Thus, numerous challenges I faced in obtaining supplies for remodeling and home repair in a remote location are no longer as relevant. But shipping charges to distant islands can still blow your mind.

- This story might seem like I hate tenants, even all of humanity. But "us versus them" is kind of the landlord paradigm, not unlike how we view opposing teams in sports—they're the ones challenging us. But there *are* good tenants. I believe there are. (I've been told.)

TABLE OF CONTENTS

LANDLADY in PARADISE

- How Not To -

Lord, Lord, Landlord!

What's worse than a landlord?

Nothing. They cramp your style and take your money. Month after month.

They show up at inopportune moments, usually on your day off, to repair stuff you didn't know was broken. They won't let you get a puppy. They move new people in upstairs just when you were finally relieved of the previous a-holes. They won't let you sublet. They always find out that you had a big party. And the only way to get your security deposit back is to scrub the oven, clean out the depths of your cabinets, and scour the laundry sink.

Sometimes a landlord won't even fix a leak dripping right by your bed, or a screen door with holes. They expect you to live with that ancient carpet until you get physically ill. And the only way to get upgrades is to spend your own money to improve *their* property. What's fair about that? They're the ones with all the money. Plus they raise the rent, or they might, any day. They might even sell the place without asking you.

Plus they have no style and they're never good-looking.

Is there anything worse than a landlord? The nicest thing to be said about them is they're an unnecessary evil. Believe me, I could totally take care of this place myself.

But, wait. Wait a minute…. Before judging the appearance of the dreaded landlord, it might be fair to ask who's gonna wear a suit and tie to mend the back fence (because the tenants got the puppy anyway). And a landlord won't likely bring over cupcakes when the neighbors across the street called at 1 a.m. because the cops were busting up your beer-pong. The landlord can hardly refund your full deposit when three different professionals had to be hired to repair the doors that got kicked and slammed during your lovers' spats. And s/he can hardly move five-star tenants in upstairs when the downstairs unit, yours, is a pigsty.

And hey, no one *aspires* to being a landlord, btw—it's a default gig. The poor soul either inherited the property or is investing as some last-ditch retirement plan.

And, actually, there IS something worse than a landlord….

Being a landlord!

Just imagine for a second being thought of or referred to the way tenants think of landlords. Just envision the stereotype. We surely all agree it's the unsexiest profession out there. I mean, did you ever dream of being a landlord? In third grade, when the teacher asked what everyone wanted to be when they grew up, did you spring from your seat to share your landlord aspirations? Were you, even as a child, captivated by the inner workings of a toilet tank? Were you asking Santa for a hand-sander?

No. And I'm sorry to say, the day-to-day is even worse than the perception. Because landlording is akin to fishing: until your catch is on the deck of the boat, i.e. tenants moved in, you don't know what you've got. All you know is that your units have to stay rented because every single day between renters costs you.

Also, landlording is *not* one of those professions that, once you're doing it, is more fun than you'd think—like maybe pole-dancing. Numerous walks of life bring you into contact with like-minded others. The lifeguard supervises other swimmers, bartenders tend other tipsy high-tippers, musicians play for other music lovers. Landlording is the opposite, far worse than you'd guess. The only thing you, as a landlord, have in common with the people residing under the roof you own is that you consider it your property and they consider it theirs. Yet you care about the property and they destroy it, you value your investment and they resent you for having an investment. And it's possibly the only job on the planet where, when you show up to work, nobody wants you there. Who wants their landlord around? "The jerk's either here to judge us or to deliver bad news. Why else would she roll up on a Tuesday afternoon (other than because she's so rich she doesn't have to work)? She's not here because she cares about the property; if she loved it so much, she'd live here herself. No, she lives in a bigger house, probably a mansion, in that other town. And that beater she drives is probably just her work car. But if she's here for no apparent reason, just happens to be in the neighborhood, that's even worse—she's up to something! Probably checking whether we moved that junk out of the back yard, or whether my brother's car is still parked here. Or she's gonna start charging us extra because my boyfriend ~~lives here~~ occasionally sleeps over."

I never wanted to be a landlord, and frankly, never enjoyed more than about ten minutes of it. Because you're not a real person as a landlord. Tenants will never offer you a cup of tea.

So, all you can do is take it in stride and accumulate one life lesson after another.

Here are some of mine.

Part 1

Buy a Fixer in Paradise ~ Live the Dream

☷ 1 ☷

Who Should Do It?

A practical couple can swing landlording relatively easily, and their rental property can fund their winter cruises. The path to landlord success is paved with such pairs. You've seen them—handy fellow with tools and truck, in tandem with secretary/interior designer. You may even wonder how they know which keys are which on that keychain, and how wealthy they must be. Sometimes the upstairs or downstairs of their own home serves as their rental, or they've inherited this rental property now feeding their retirement. The secret sauce is that they're in it together.

LESSON : Landlords do best in couples.

So, if you've got a man's man hubby whose nickname is "I Got This," you'll probably only be tasked with placing potted plants by the front door of your rental. And if you're a girl's girl who books manicures weeks in advance and never leaves home without your face on, you'll probably be delegated just nominal chores like placing the ads or paying the property tax, as Hubs handles the heavy lifting. And maybe you'll sashay between Lowe's and Sherwin-Williams, choosing cabinet handles and paint colors, "Let's see, should the master bedroom be *Creme de la Creme* or *Puff de la Puff?*"

However, there are also droves of less perfectly suited landlords, for whom owning rental property is strictly about income. Like know-how guys with deep pockets and extra time. But nearly none—especially single females knowing bupkis about home maintenance or management—choose landlording out of sheer desperation.

When I bought my Santa Monica condo at age forty-eight, and phoned my dad to announce I'd closed escrow, he said, "Welcome to the middle class," and wasn't being sarcastic. It was then I realized property ownership is a privilege—you finally have something to fall back on, something to barter later for health care. (Plus, whew, you no longer have a landlord.)

But it didn't take long to figure out that, so what if you own a home, you can't trade it for anything because you *live* in it. In terms of amassing assets, owning just one property doesn't actually advance you. You've got to secure something ELSE for those looming later years.

Okay, many have something set up—pensions, 401K's, adequate Social Security, maybe an inheritance or divorce settlement—and many do or will depend on spouses and/or children. But one way or another, everyone needs a plan for the senior decades, other than purchasing lottery tickets. Otherwise, as dawns on most everyone in midlife, we ~~may~~ will hit the wall.

But having been a freelancer my whole life, putting freedom and independence before monetary well-being, I didn't have it in me to now become an anesthesiologist or get a law degree. Though anything would be better than working at Starbucks with white hair, I really couldn't think of what to do. I'm hopeless at nine-to-five, bad at stocks, dumb at day-trading, horrible at gambling, and afraid to be a flight attendant. I was already late to the party as a massage therapist (hardly a get-rich pursuit anyway) and the clock was ticking.

Thus, I began eerily tabulating that if you're not financially set, and you're spouse- and kid-free, with no windfall coming your way, and you entertain some vision of growing old…then owning rental property is *mandatory*. With my future Social Security slated at around $474 a month,* my inner financial coach was wagging an index finger, "You better get your hands on some real estate, babe, cuz you're in your early fifties with no plan."

It's just a fact that the best place for an average Joe to sock their money is into rental property. So, as it became clear that my Social Security wouldn't even cover food and gas, I concluded that obtaining *another* property was my only course of action. And I started poking around for affordable property in Santa Monica and Venice, where I lived.

But why would a single woman with no construction skills consider a profession that's at best unsexy and at worst grueling? Three reasons:

1. Real estate is normally a long-term play. (That's why it best fits mature investors.) Rental property is probably *the* most sure-fire bet for long-term prosperity if you've got enough years to see it to fruition. And once you've committed to a property, if you're willing to do the work, that financial opportunity, though never guaranteed, is actually available to *anyone*. You don't need a degree, won't have a boss or anyone telling you what to do, there's no roulette wheel spinning, no

stock market fluctuations, not even much actual financial risk…if you don't mind waiting.

The case for doing it is strong. Aside from paying down your mortgage with the rent from one, two, or more units every month—often providing excess funds—your property value goes up also. So, theoretically, you've got two income streams. And even if real estate goes down for a while, a decent property will invariably bounce back up over time.

Pretty much everyone's on board with the concept that if you want to make money, you gotta work. (If not, this book is way over your head.) And being a landlord truly isn't the *worst* job. You're not going down the mines or re-wiring power lines in the blazing sun. It's not nine-to-five, you're not on the night shift, you're not on some tedious assembly line, and you're not juggling two jobs to make ends meet. There are even lulls where little is required of you for weeks, even months, at a time. Plus lots of landlords keep their day jobs.

On the other hand, unlike the above mentioned professions, if you get fed up with landlording, you can't simply toss in the towel.

LESSON : Understand the nature of "long-term." The envisioned rewards that inspire a rental property purchase won't be arriving in a year or two, or even four or five. You could be in this for decades. So if you crave freedom and travel, or thrive on exciting new ventures, if you have a consuming career, or family demands, or creative passions, then owning rental property will not only detract from those pastimes, but possibly cancel them out for a chunk of your life!

So what should you buy, and where?

A) The property should be in either a good location or one that's up-and-coming.

B) Don't buy something nobody else wants just because it's cheap. If nobody wants it now, there's a chance nobody'll want it when you're ready to sell. (Unless you're in on some community secret, like you got wind they'll be dismantling that pesky nuclear power plant.) *LESSON :* Buy in a promising neighborhood. In a funky location, the renters you'll attract may not be so savory.

Also, since you'll be spending time there yourself, don't select a pocket of misery that no amount of energy or funding can resuscitate. Pick a place that, *if you had to live there yourself,* it wouldn't be half bad. You never know, you might well find yourself living there for a while…especially once it's renovated. A lot can happen in ten or twenty years. You could get divorced, you could choose to downsize, your millennial freeloader could move out…. Pick a property with enough redeeming qualities that you could conceivably spend time there yourself.

LESSON : In Hawai'i (I don't know about other places), it's the law that all landlords must live on the island where their rental property is situated. So check the local laws before you buy!

2. Owning rental property is an opportunity to make the world nicer. You might salvage a wreck of a house. For artsy types, architectural types, construction types, or entrepreneurial singles or couples, there's pleasure in proving what TLC can do. If you like restoring wood floors, re-doing walls, upgrading counters; if you love replacing doors, adore landscaping, or if remodeling porches makes your heart sing; if you like knobs and window treatments, lighting fixtures, sinks, and tubs, the landlord gig is packed with projects and logistical equations to solve. If you're okay with sweat equity,

property renovation can be emotionally fulfilling. Though dealing day to day with amped-up workers might be trying, the pride of restoring a beat-up property will endure and the satisfaction can't be taken from you.

3. Real estate is not pie in the sky, it's *real*. Though from the moment you apply the finishing touches to your property and rent it out, wear and tear begin tarnishing your labor of love and everything grows rapidly less glamorous, it's still your property. If you can hang in and weather the landlord storms— plus inflation, recession, natural disasters, stock market crashes, terrorism, pandemics, political disparity, and more— you continue owning the ground it sits upon and having tenant income. You can plant things. You can harvest fruit from your trees to eat or sell. And when the world goes to hell in a hand-basket, as it now officially has, you have something *real*. You can live on the land, let your children or aging parents live there. On your land, you can enjoy the natural splendor of the world, lie in the grass and gaze at the stars at night (though few landlords do, I'm not sure why). And when you plant your trees and watch them flower and grow, then a decade or two roll by and you've got hundreds of gorgeous tangerines, you can have moments of love and gratitude that only property owners experience.

And…someday…you can sell that property for *real* money. Hopefully, a bundle more than you paid for it.

It's not all misery and drama.

* I'm pleased to report that, over time, I was able to radically increase my Social Security. :)

Suzys' Advice

Advice of #1 Suzy

I had the condo—a great investment, because I actually DID know a community secret when I bought it, that rent control was ending soon and values would likely soar. So I soon had equity there, to conceivably use for a modest down payment on a second property. Maybe I could snag some little ghetto house and rent it out. Then one day it would be worth more and I'd sell it.

So I found a slummy little house for sale in Venice and called the realtor on the sign. Suzy Frank popped right over. "Why are you looking at these houses in the ghetto?" Realtors need to know your intentions.

"I'm gonna invest. I'm gonna be a landlord."

"If you buy a house with just one unit, like a one-family dwelling, you put tenants in there and they pay the rent, and that pays your mortgage, but that's it," she said. "There's really no *income,* since the tenants only pay the mortgage, nothing more. Well, possibly a few bucks a month, but that would go toward repairs, because you'll always have maintenance. With one rental unit, you don't *make* any money."

My brow furrowed. Where was she going with this? Having convinced myself that buying a rental house was my sole solution, was Suzy nixing it?

She continued, "Sometimes one unit won't even bring in enough to cover all your maintenance, property taxes, and insurance. In that case, the only profit you'll ever see is when you finally sell the place, at which time, hopefully, it's worth more than you bought it for."

"You're bumming me out."

"But that's the reality," she shrugged. "Even with tenants covering the mortgage, all the maintenance and big repairs through the years—like new roofs and paint jobs—are on you. So…unless you get a really good deal on something and flip it, you don't *make* any money with a one-unit house until you sell it."

And there were ZERO deals to be had on the west side of Los Angeles. "Oh well," I sighed.

"But," said Suzy, "that's why you have to have at least two units. Then your first unit pays the mortgage and your second unit pays *you*."

I let that sink in….

"Oh-h-h-h." I probably should've figured that out myself, but this angle had never entered my mind. "But…" I stammered, "…then you're *really a landlord*."

"You're gonna really be a landlord anyway if you buy a house. You might as well have two units instead of one." She was matter-of-fact.

I had to blink a few times, but it was clear that, due to my allergies about slaving away at a regular job, owning a two-unit rental property was my only bankable, long-term prospect. "That makes total sense," I had to admit. "Like, why would I buy one unit? I have to buy two."

This was one of those moments when a door flings open. There and then, my entire outlook, in fact my life itself, pivoted. And I never looked back.

But rental property in Southern California, especially a two-unit place, was beyond my means.

Advice of #2 Suzy

Hurricane 'Iniki had demolished the island of Kaua'i in 1992, and the island went off the radar for so long…that it was…completely forgotten. Then, ten years later, when it bleeped back onto the screen, real estate prices there weren't yet up to speed with Maui and O'ahu, where the focus had been the whole previous decade.

Suzy #2, a producer in LA who had optioned a screenplay I wrote, got wind about real estate on Kaua'i being unusually affordable at this one fluke moment around 2002. This sharp little Suzy also discovered that the "no doc" loans currently on offer (with 20% down, you could get a mortgage without any proof of steady employment), could even be obtained by artists! You just needed some cash. And since Suzy and her husband had some, by securing a no doc loan, they snapped up a two-bedroom plantation house on Kaua'i.

But Suzy's move to Hawai'i threw me, "Suzy, how are we gonna make the movie?"

"Oh, we're still gonna do it, I'll just be on Kaua'i. But I'll have my same phone number and no one needs to know I'm not in LA."

"Hm…I'm not convinced…."

"No, no, don't worry!"

But I did worry because the screenplay meant everything to me. So after Suzy moved, I flew over to verify that our project was still a go. Or had she had swapped out Hollywood (and me) for the hot tropics?

It was the latter. Suzy's husband had lucrative work on O'ahu, so she was now blissfully restoring her new home and living aloha. Though she gave fleeting lip service to the screenplay, it was abundantly clear that everything about the Mainland was in her wake.

Still, Suzy #2 alerted me to this freak moment when precious Hawai'i real estate was not just reasonable, but anyone with 20% cash down, even freelancers, could get loans. Heretofore unheard of!

In light of the normal out-of-reach real estate prices in Hawai'i and stringent criteria for loan qualification, I'd never imagined owning property there. Nor had there been one moment of my adult life when artsy types could get mortgages. But now, while visiting Suzy on Kaua'i, I started browsing around for another condo to perhaps purchase as a vacation rental.

But with the market smokin' hot and prices surging upwards by the day, I'd have to move fast to seize this opportunity. With no partner or kids to consider though, I was positioned for swift unilateral decisions.

Thus, quite spontaneously, instead of a condo, I bought a three-bedroom plantation house. Not as a rental property, but to live in! Hey, the movie wasn't going to happen. And as a massage therapist and yoga instructor, I could find work in Hawai'i. Shucks, I'd just sell my California condo and move to Kaua'i!

The transplant, of course, would throw my whole show akimbo. But…next thing I knew, everything was being reconfigured to accommodate my exotic new geography.

New Plan

I had $200,000 equity in my Santa Monica condo by then. The plan was to now sell it, use $100,000 as down payment for my Kaua'i house and hold the other $100,000 for down payment on a rental property (with two units) that would also be on Kaua'i. "But," that inner financial coach wagged that finger again, "if you're after another Hawaiian property, it's now or never, kid. These loans won't last, nor will prices stay in reach like this."

So, still living on the Mainland while lining up my ducks for the overseas move, I'd have to go on line to find a Kaua'i fixer-upper—some dive I could convert into two units—before prices shot up.

I began my Internet search.

LESSON : It's advised that your rental property be within an hour's drive of your residence.

The Yellow Paper

The word got out and a massive real estate boom hit Kaua'i. Houses sold in just days, leaving hardly any inventory. So, partly because my criteria were so specific, my on-line search continued for months. My Kaua'i realtor, Carter, was also searching, and also coming up empty-handed.

It was now over a year after buying my first house, and the big move slated for the end of the month. Then, after five months of combing the Internet, and just a week before my flight, I saw a listing for a five-bedroom/two-bath house that a) met my budget, b) had a floor plan conducive to dividing into two units, and c) was ten minutes from my other house. Having taken so-o-o long to find something potentially workable, my relief was palpable. And though it was in a working-class neighborhood, I had expected to make concessions due to my limited finances. I'd also have to build a second kitchen, amongst other tall orders. But still, having nearly given up, I knew this was my last chance to own a two-unit property close to my other house.

I phoned Carter, who nipped straight over to check it out. And the next day, he sent pictures along with an email, "I think this house could, indeed, be converted to suit your needs." But he added, "And since you'll be here soon, you should put in an offer."

I'd sold my condo, but that $100,000 designated for the rental property down payment had somehow dwindled down to $65,000, as inevitably happens with cash in hand. But I still had *just* enough to plunk down for this house.

Viewing Carter's photos, the layout really did look appropriate. But the house was pretty shabby.… And my overriding sentiment wasn't excitement, but, "*Eeeek,* what am I getting into?" Was this the best move I'd ever make, or the worst? The uncertainty had me quaking in my boots. So I phoned my island handyman, Homer, to pitch him my scheme. Someone would have to bring some experience to this venture.

Carter, meanwhile, pressed, "I think you can make the house into what you want, but you better make an offer because the market's so hot."

"But I'm still on the Mainland…."

"You're coming in a few days. And once you're here, if you decide you don't want it, you can bail after the inspection. That's perfectly legal. You have fifteen days after making your offer to opt out."

I was quiet. Put in an offer? I hadn't even seen the place.

"If you wait until you get here, you're probably gonna lose it. If I were you, I'd go ahead and make my offer."

"Okay," I sighed, "offer them $5000 under asking." Even though the place was a shambles, I sensed $5000 was all the wiggle room I had.

"Done. I'll keep you posted."

I trusted Carter. I sort of had to! Fortunately, he was likable, humorous, amenable, hardworking, and knew the trade. He himself actually owned *twenty-one* rental properties on the island. (That he was a slumlord didn't surface until later, when he shared with me his cost-cutting tactics for remodeling.)

He now estimated I'd need about $20,000 to whip this house into shape. Not totally terrifying since I already had borrowing equity on my first house, that had already climbed in value. Weak in the knees, I phoned Homer again. Only with him as my right hand could I proceed. "Homer, if I buy this second house, are you on board with the renovation? I absolutely need you." Little did I know, it's a handyman's or construction worker's dream to have a naive new homeowner ask you to lead the charge on a giant construction project.

"I can do that," Homer agreed—though as much out of kindness, in his case, as opportunism. Then, after viewing the house, he, too, estimated twenty grand for repairs.

A New Life

When crawling onto tenuous monetary limbs and/or pursuing outlandish goals, blind courage is sometimes all you've got.

Arriving on Kaua'i with my cat and all my possessions, Carter met the plane and escorted me straight to the house, where he'd scheduled a viewing. The current owner and family were home, so this maiden visit to the stunningly lackluster premises was too superficial for comfort. The good news was that the layout *could* accommodate my vision, the bad news was that the place was worse than I'd surmised, the overall condition shameful.

Eeeeek! What to do? And all by my lonesome? With no experience? On a remote island where I knew practically no one?

But it had taken me so long to find this, prices were still soaring, and these miraculous loans could suddenly vanish. Plus I was fifty-freakin'-four.

Carter reassured me I had fifteen days to complete my inspection and then, should I choose, still back out. "And I've got an inspector for you, a great guy named Frank. And he's reasonable, he'll only charge you $400."

The inspection would shed realistic light on the costs of restoration—particularly those that didn't meet the untrained eye—as well as the complexities of transforming the house into two units. So in the last days before possible deed signing, I was waiting with baited breath for the inspection and the final word. Comforted that this inspector was vetted by Carter, I met Frank two days later at the property.

LESSON : It's probably not customary for a buyer to participate in the inspection. But it's permissible. And I highly recommend being present for it.

Frankie Boy, congenial-bordering-on-lackadaisical, wasn't taking his gig too seriously though. In fact, this was just his side hustle, it turned out. Our first fifteen minutes, he rattled around clicking light switches and turning faucets on and off, then for the remaining fifteen, I called the shots as he trailed along puppy-like, checking things off on his clipboard. I had to beg him to go onto the roof and to worm under the house—

both efforts more gymnastic than he bargained for. Was this guy even certified?

And when we did climb onto the roof, at my insistence, Frank offered to hold the ladder while I went first, then pinched my butt while climbing up behind me. Then giggled at my astonishment.

LESSON : Don't hire an inspector referred by your realtor. An honest assessment can't be expected from anyone working for Team Realtor, because quashing sales won't win him more gigs. So this person may not even thoroughly inspect the place, or worse, may *withhold* from you legitimate concerns, even hideous truths, about the property.

But such littleness didn't cross my mind.

When we finished bumbling around, I lobbied Frank to fill out his paperwork in a Japanese tea house around the corner so I wouldn't have to wait another day or longer for his report. He, of course, wanted to get back to me tomorrow, but I pleaded and offered to buy lunch.

On floor cushions at the tea house, we munched on rice concoctions as Frank filled out his forms and I impatiently waited. Finally he came up with his conclusive estimate for the renovation: $20,000.

At this, I was elated. Carter, Homer, and Frank all concurred! And $20,000 was manageable. I could do it!

Still, hesitancy was riding shotgun, a stubborn lump lodged in my throat…. The more I thought about what I was getting into—owning two fixer-uppers all by myself and taking on unfathomable debt—the more anxiety welled within. I'd never tackled anything of this magnitude, especially on leveraged funds, in an unknown profession, and on an island 3000 miles from all support. I wasn't a carpenter, didn't own a truck, and was a total novice about not only construction but everything pertaining to the world's most remote archipelago. My guardian angels were now waving red flags, even jumping up and down, *"You can still back out!"*

"But wait a minute…." my bigger self confronted them. "Is this just FEAR blocking me from greater destiny?"

Of course it was! I caught myself. What else could it be? (This was the era when believing in oneself to absurd extremes was all the rage, and all fear was considered just bullshit.) "It's gotta be just stupid ol' fear. Yup, that's what it is. I'm just afraid of The Unknown."

To fortify the more enlightened perspective and to bolster my courage, the day before the dreaded deed signing, I took a yellow note pad to a North Shore beach and plunked down in the sand to dismantle my concerns, one by one. "By writing out my fears," I reasoned, "I can then release them to the universe." I glanced skyward for some kind of nod.

"Or…" quaked my scared self, "when you see them spelled out on paper, they'll freak you out so totally, you'll come to your senses and opt out of this folly."

As the sun dropped to the water line, and sunset colors tried to distract me, I solemnly listed every possible thing that could go wrong—from the financial side, to the construction side, to the tenant side, to the living-in-Hawai'i side, to the getting-in-way-too-deep side, even to the blindside side. Fear and consternation covered the page….then a second page.

I did not like what I saw. Instead of feeling relieved and empowered like I was supposed to, I had now identified *even more* fears on top of my existing ones. Itemizing one's trepidations, I discovered, doesn't neutralize suffocating angst. And "releasing it all to the universe" wasn't flying too high either. So I just sat numbly in the sand as the sun melted into the sea....

But finally, with resolve, I folded the two yellow pages and filed them away as Plain Old Fear. "You twit, you can do anything you really put your mind to. *Sat Nam.*" I stood up and brushed myself off. My intrepid self won the day. I would proceed with the purchase. And I'd bury this list in a drawer, not to peek at again for a good while—knowing that when I finally revisited these fears, I'd laugh out loud at how scared, small-minded, and wussy I'd been.

A Yogic Aside (Sat Nam)

Opportunities don't always flaunt themselves. They're brief interludes where we feel a subtle or dramatic shift. Or pauses where we scrutinize ourselves and perceive some need for change. There's a cosmic whisper and we actually hear it.

When I was about thirty-five, I remember standing in my small apartment on Venice Beach as I prepared to go roller skating. There was a moment of unexpected clarity that day. I'd recently been at odds with my own mind, doubting my perspectives. But simply and suddenly, I realized that it was okay for me to...*be me.* This person was fun, this person had good intentions, this person was strong and intended to survive. Though different from others, this person was a decent companion—bankable, viable, accountable, gutsy, and game. Thus, it made no sense for me to question my own personality, instincts, or intentions, or to not be my own friend. I'd been dealt a good hand, I had my groove, and my best bet going forward was to live it up within my own quirky soul.

From that moment right up to this one, I've liked myself. And stayed loyal.

Those thoughts back then also helped me understand the meaning of 'Sat Nam,' a mantra I'd been chanting in yoga classes for years, though not really comprehending (probably because my teachers didn't comprehend the meaning either). I knew the definition and translation from Sanskrit, 'true self,' but didn't understand what it meant to *my life*, or how to apply it.

But the irony of self love, and why people shy away from the concept, is because they fear self love is vanity, or hubris, or ego…. But self love isn't arrogant or something we exhibit. It's merely being one's own friend—an acquired skill.

So I thank yoga for teaching me Sat Nam. It's so important. It gives one solace and confidence.

☷☷ ☷☷ ☷☷ ☷☷

We closed escrow.

Because the house was such a hunk-o'-junk, I ended up getting the price down another ten grand. And I got my no doc, 4%, thirty-year, adjustable-rate loan for about $250,000.

Under the American credo called "leveraging," I then stepped across the divide that separates nice working folk from over-extended business types. And "over-extended" would be my theme song for a *long* time. And though there's nothing illegal about having debt or home equity lines of credit, what I didn't know yet was that when you're in way too deep (like can't-sleep deep), unforeseens can be crippling. The longer the limb you go out on, the more likely it will break…and the greater the karmic load you'll have to bear.

Owning this rental property would dominate my next sixteen years—hardly how I'd envisioned life under the swaying palms. But despite cost and stress, I had no choice—this strategy alone could doctor a dubious future.

Bright and early the morning after closing, Homer and I reported to work.

The General Contractor

From day one after signing the deed, you're paying mortgage, insurance, property taxes, and utilities. Empty houses with mortgages drain you *each passing day,* so getting renters is top priority. Therefore, 150% of your time and energy must go toward readying your place. And where, previously, you've been *paid* to work like a maniac, you're now *paying* to work like a maniac, often thousands per week.

My new job—sixteen hours a day, seven days a week—was to transform a three-bedroom/one-bath home with a one-bedroom/one-bath extension, into two attractive units with separate entrances, including one new kitchen. But my inexperience, my gender, and my expectations about Paradise began backfiring straight away. Without training, truck, tools, equipment, partner, or mentor to confab with or vent to, I had boarded a runaway train. (Raising quadruplets with no spouse might be an analogy.)

On a sizable construction project, it's standard procedure to hire a General Contractor, or GC, to coordinate and supervise everything, taking you off the hook (except financially). Experienced in construction and with a can-do air, the GC hires and manages workers, and handles the sequencing of tasks and procurement of materials. He'll strive to keep your troubles (and your participation) to a minimum. GCs expect you to let them do as much as possible, believing they're doing you a favor. And for most people, they are.

But you pay handsomely for someone to babysit your project. And since the General Contractor's wages are usually buried somewhere within your mountain of expenses, you never quite tally up the outrageous extent of it! But believing there's way more to the renovation than homeowners alone can handle, most simply factor the GC into their overall costs. Plus lots have full-time jobs and must defer to the muscle-man with the fancy wheels and "expert'" demeanor. And truth be told, if you don't mind a) paying through the nose, and b) being second fiddle or even no fiddle, hiring a GC makes sense.

I wasn't comfortable with "a" or "b," so didn't initially give the GC issue any thought—partly because I'd never heard of them and partly because, when I did, their fees were staggering. I figured a GC wasn't offering anything I couldn't figure out on my own, one way or another.... I've never been a yes-man anyway, and always sort of *a la carte.* I decided to just have specialist workers perform the zillion tasks ahead and consult with each about the situation *du jour.*

But the GC issue is substantial and must be considered. It's about both know-how and control. *LESSON :* If you're super hands-on, want your own creative stamp on the project, or want your say in every little thing, you'll need to either BE the GC or find one who doesn't mind constantly communicating with you and implementing your wishes.

I never regretted being my own GC, because having just made this heart-stopping purchase, the last thing I wanted (though desperately needed) was some smooth dude making executive decisions about my property, on my Home Depot card. And I avoided a ton of expense, plus a lot of consultation and possible friction

Demanding as it was being the GC, a lot of it IS common sense, and all of it learnable. Still, I encountered a maelstrom of construction challenges, rogue workers, overages, depleted reserves, and ulcer-inducing shock as costs soared and things-that-could-go-wrong did. Newly identified items like rafter-tails, fascia, and elbow joints devoured my hours, as a colorful cast filed through the job-site, each with his pickup, idiosyncratic work habits, inflated ego, and judgements about my renovation concepts and "boss" qualifications.

It turned out the house I purchased was practically a tear-down! And fixing something that's shot to hell can, not infrequently, cost more than just starting over. In some circumstances, repair is actually futile. So from the get-go, my renovation was fraught with financial overages, changes of plans, and often having to tear things out and start over anyway. But I held to my belief that property on Kaua'i was worth more than maybe any material thing on the planet and, should I survive, my investment would one day bear fruit.

But those first few years, I was so out of my league, I wouldn't even admit my harebrained enterprise to anyone. That this little massage therapist/yoga teacher owned two houses on Kaua'i sounded…highly unlikely, if not fabricated. So after the renovation, when I got back to my yoga and massage work—that, by comparison, was effortless, relaxing, and fun—I kept my tycoon side under wraps. But my debt and paying it down, were crazy real.

And I'm really lucky no soothsayer tipped me off that I'd spend the next TEN YEARS twisted like a pretzel from responsibility, monetary pressure, loneliness, and commitment to a long-term plan that would've been a stretch for anyone. Not a week went by, for ten straight years, that I didn't ask myself, "Should I just sell?"

But I never did. Despite owing $532,000 at the low point, plus the additional setback of the seven-year recession that would barrel in—my two properties were always worth more than my debt. So, always technically in the black, I could hold to that distant mirage of eventual security. As long as I continued landlording, that income, plus increasing property values, were real.

Even many years into it, I never regretted straining my skillset and accounting to the max. And I remained in the black for the duration. Mine was what they call "good debt" (though it didn't feel that great). And I lived in Paradise. And I got to fully transform two neglected plantation houses into sweet Hawaiian homes.

Part II

Fix the Fixer

≡ 5 ≡
The Process

Getting Started

Homer readily informed me that he and I alone couldn't cut it; we needed at least one more bigger, tougher, experienced guy. So I was recruiting.

In November 2004, bulletin boards and newspaper ads were where one found workers. And on our local health food store bulletin board, a construction worker had an ad up. With all the letters squared off in caps, even the penmanship looked constructed. (He may have posted it with nails instead of thumb tacks.) I called the guy, who agreed to come by the house the next day.

Dave rolled up in his bronze pickup and hopped out. A human 4-by-4, functionality defined him. But he wasn't macho, and actually came across as attentive, bright, and polite—in that Kansas way that makes you forget that most Americans aren't like that.

As I showed him the house and spelled out my plans, he nodded his way through the rooms, and offered his take on what would be required, including details no novice would've remotely considered. After twenty minutes, Dave declared outright that he was my champion, worry no more, let's get started, this job was just what he wanted.

$25 an hour was the going rate at that time and what I expected to pay my workers. Dave wanted $35, but assured me he was worth it, knew how to do things, had all the tools, and would work hard. Sensing how much I'd rely on him, his request was reasonable—he really was exactly who Homer and I needed. And with time of the essence, Dave's eagerness was a Godsend.

I felt fortunate signing him on. And we three set sail that same day. Dave would be powering through the big jobs, while Homer and I bustled from chore to chore, picking up the slack.

Dave actually lobbied hard the first ten days or so to be my GC, but I didn't cave. I knew that, when snafus hit, I'd be the one fielding all the accountability anyway.

The second morning, as Dave pulled into the drive, I couldn't ignore a red-haired gal in the back of his pickup. I moved forward to make her acquaintance, to which Dave said she would wait in the truck while he worked. "No," I shook my head, "she shouldn't stay in the truck. I love dogs. She can come inside, she can be part of this."

Rosie melted me at first sight. Part Rhodesian Ridgeback and part Golden Lab, with her heart on her sleeve, she instantly let me know the feeling was mutual. And throughout Dave's tenure, Rosie was on the job with us. (She had an inexplicable, growly thing where she'd bare her teeth on occasion for no clear reason, but it never led to anything, and Dave dismissed it as generic dog unrest.)

On our to-do list—all to be renovated, repaired, restored and/or outfitted—were five bedrooms; two bathrooms (one to be re-plumbed); two kitchens (one to be built from scratch and plumbed in an empty room, that also needed a new ceiling and a window where there wasn't one); two porches; all new wiring and lighting fixtures throughout the house; new flooring on every square foot; eleven new windows, including two more that I'd carve into existing walls; all new interior and exterior doors; and all new cabinetry and vanities. Then would come the cosmetic side: painting all interior walls and ceilings; buying new appliances; painting the exterior of the house and porches; and clearing up the mess of a yard and landscaping it. Plus the roof wasn't draining right and the rafter tails were termited out.

Some projects could be done simultaneously, so I'd bring in this guy for plumbing, that guy for electricity, this one for ceilings, that one for landscaping. I had a door dude, a roof dude, and everyone in between. And though, practically speaking, there were numerous tasks I could perform myself—painting, laying tile, taking down walls, landscaping, hammering nails, sanding, spackling—as Master of Ceremonies, I was supervising the whole circus all day long, organizing and outlining everything to take place, hiring and overseeing assignments, buying materials and supplying everyone with what they needed, and examining results so we could proceed with what came next. And if I didn't run out to fetch the new blade for a saw, or more paint, or sandpaper, or nails, I had to pay someone else by the hour just to drive to the Home Depot. So even though I'd expected to assist with the labor, every time I was about to knuckle under, someone would flag me down and I was back to troubleshooting and decision making. Plus, I had to constantly confer with Dave and Homer about what I wanted vis-a-vis how, or if, it could happen, and how.

"Hawaiian houses are held together by termites holding hands," is a phrase coined by realtors and homeowners here—especially places like mine, where the previous family password had been "neglect" or "LasVegas_here_we_come!" And one of my earlier rude awakenings was when, assessing the extent of the termite damage, we were poking around the rafter tails.

For those unfamiliar with construction, rafters are the 2-by-6 wood beams that form the A-frame holding up a roof. In an attic, these lengthy planks can be seen extending from the roof apex all the way down to the outer walls of the house, then continuing outside where they hold up the eaves. Rafter "tails" are the visible ends of the beams underneath the eaves or overhang.

Bizarrely though, I turned out to be the lone person on the planet with damaged rafter tails…and was to discover they're a) practically impossible to fix or replace, and b) NO ONE knows how to do it. (Fab Frank overlooked this trifle.)

So, how DOES one cut the end off a rafter and install another tail without destroying the whole beam and/or threatening the integrity of the roof? I asked everyone at Home Depot and every handyman or carpenter friend I could track down from my past. To this day, over twenty years later, I still can't recommend any straight solution for troubled tails.

For us, it became a case-by-case undertaking, each tail its own perplexity. Some we patched with spackle or Bondo, some we shored up with new wood pieces, some we "sistered" with more wood, one or two we cut off by climbing up inside the attic crawl-space, then slid in a new piece of wood from way up there.

But, disturbingly, since none of my guys had ever encountered this quandary before, we lost real time batting the issue around and experimenting—every twenty-minute pow-wow costing greenbacks.

That's when I learned that my male compadres didn't know "everything," that each generally had a specialty or two, and that my common sense actually trumped theirs on occasion. Thus, in the months to come, there were times when, despite flak from the fellas, I had to put my foot down and just call it. Because no matter what any of them said or believed, no matter how much experience they had, I was footing the bill, I was the owner, and I would be at this house long after we'd forgotten each other's names. So when I felt strongly about something, even if my reasons seemed whimsical or unorthodox to them, I learned to honor my intuition and hold firm.

Next on our list were the termite-ridden windows. "Let's just repair the originals and keep the plantation style," was my thinking. Fixing windows seemed fairly rudimentary, probably not too complex or expensive….

But not so fast. How badly damaged are they? Remember, replacing is sometimes easier, even less costly, than repairing.

We decided the eight primary windows of the front unit had to be put out of their misery and replaced by larger new ones. But the look of the house would change, so I had to be sensitive and consistent in choosing the style of new windows. But out in mid-Pacific in 2004, "choosing" was rarely part of the equation—you'd take what was available. Because waiting six weeks for special orders, i.e. everything you'd prefer, was, for seat-o'-the-pants projects like mine, out of the question.

We also needed the mastery to install these windows. But Dynamo Dave loved nothing more than assignments promising he'd sweat for hours or days, so was delighted to take them on. "And while we're at it," I showed him the three additional spaces I'd designated on interior walls, "let's put in three more new ones in these spots." ("And while we're at it," are supposedly the five most expensive words you can utter during a remodel.)

Dave jumped in with purpose. But his approach soon struck everyone on the job as overkill, and guys were tipping me off, "You don't need to build bomb-shelter frames like he's doing. Installing a new window should only take a few hours."

"Dave," I finally said, "it shouldn't take five days to put in a window."

"I'm doing a really good job."

True, his work was solid and near perfect, so I only nudged him a couple of times.

His final stance was, "When the hurricane comes, and all the other houses in the neighborhood are gone, your house will still be standing." Probably correct, but I was finding out that new windows only require careful measuring, building a quick, basic frame, then snapping in the new pre-fab window.

But Dave knew I didn't know that. And his elaborate installations were my first indicator that he wasn't above workin' me....

Pleasing Aesthetics

Though few homeowners are willing to pop for additional expense, pleasing aesthetics enhance property values. But more importantly, they made me happy because I couldn't bear looking at, or owning, anything tacky or chintzy. Hence, slews of money-saving suggestions and shortcuts were lost on me, and many of my choices not only cost extra but sparked resistance from my crew. "Wendy, it's a rental! Why are you making it so nice? If it was *your* house, then it would make sense, but this is a *rental.*"

"It IS my house," I'd reply. "I own it. Yes, I'm making it nice, but there are some nice people out there and that's who I want to rent to."

Even now, a small fortune and years later, I remain pleased I made the house beautiful. Because every single time I'd set foot in either the front or back unit—through all the years that followed—to inspect or clean or repair or meet with tenants—I was soothed and reassured: everything was lovely. I constantly admired our fine work—the bamboo floors in the living room, the extra windows, the finish-carpentry details, the flowering plants you could see from inside, the travertine for the kitchen floor and terracotta in the bathroom. I never regretted the pastel tints on bedroom walls, the elegant lighting, or the custom woodwork where it was totally unnecessary but enhanced everything. These were the features potential tenants always commented on, along with the feel-good vibe of every square foot of the place. (And I did find fantastic bargains, at the lumber store 'bone yard,' and just by always asking about options and alternatives.)

In the final analysis, everything we did, we did well. I didn't tolerate shabby work—if it wasn't right, it wasn't right. I'd even repay workers to redo things. And by the end of the project, I had two standing mantras that I'd recommend to anyone supervising a renovation. *LESSON :* "Do it once and do it right" and "We work clean." Towards the end, I'd always communicate these "house rules" to new guys coming on the job.

And that consistent quality was what, much later, gave me confidence to only sell the house for the high price it deserved.

6

How to Get an Ulcer

Once upon a time, my early mornings involved an inviting notebook and perfectly doctored coffee. Now 7 a.m. meant meeting my beefy crew (some wet from surfing) and commencing my day with, "Here's your plywood. Do we have enough? Here's the wood glue you needed that I got last night from the Depot. Here's your spackle. You need more tape? Was that the right measurement we took yesterday? No, I haven't seen your tape measure."

In the evenings, no less than five a week, I attended the Home Depot 'School,' where I'd consult with employees there and purchase wagonloads of supplies. Paid by the hour by the store, those workers were mellow and happy to help. Every night I'd arrive around 6, and stay 'til closing at 9, confabulating with the electric guy, the plumbing guy, the wood guy, the trim guy, the window guy, all of whom I knew by name and who tutored me. "How do I install track lighting? Do I need an electrician? Can I patch the bathtub or do I have to get a new one? How do I fix a kitchen faucet? What are the advantages or disadvantages of bi-fold doors? What's a piano hinge?"

Truly, I couldn't have accomplished that renovation without that night school! I even recruited part-time workers from there. Yes, I shelled out ridiculous sums (often winning two-year loans with no interest), and could never quite believe that the buyer of all these sinks and toilets, lumber, windows, doors, and buckets of plaster could possibly be me.

Despite Dave's knowledge and energy, and Homer's loyalty and flexibility, I remained painfully alone in spending *thousands,* with no end in sight. And where I'd bargained for $20,000 in repairs, we blew past that in no time. And though the "experts" had estimated one month, we toiled for five— because you can't just not replace cringe-worthy light fixtures and stained thresholds, nor tear-ass to the finish line when you've still got floors to repair, drywall to go up, vanities to install. The whole project didn't cost $20,000, but $80,000, not to mention collecting no rent for five months. I was eatin' money for breakfast, lunch, and dinner, along with four-inch construction nails, and cryin' all the way *from* the bank.

LESSON : Understand your risk. Even if your property seems an excellent bet, your trajectory won't be a predictable graph.

Still, the actual process of building and renovating isn't entirely woeful. It's interesting, educational, and something you can throw your mind and body into with a vengeance. Plus it's ensemble work—nice when you have the right group.

And I was always conscious that, though not knowing what I was doing, *I wanted to do this.*

Surging forward, the plan was now to just work non-stop. My clipboard was an extension of my arm. On it were "to-do" columns: jobs for each day and each worker, supplies to pick up, "still-to-do" chores, "mustn't forgets," plus all my own tasks and errands. Almost daily, I'd start a fresh page that would fill up in hours. And the only way to sooth my anxieties was to prayerfully reinstate my purpose, "If I can endure the stress, soon I'll be collecting rent from two units. And someday the property value should go up. So even though I owe a ton, I'll probably get it back someday…and then some."

Around that time is when the ulcer developed.

Christmas came. Because my mother had died young, I never missed a Christmas with my wonderful aging dad on Long Island. I now needed ten days with him.

I'd leave Dave in charge, knowing he'd work dutifully—partly because he'd proven that and partly because he had little else going on. (He'd confided that his own parental relationship was subpar.) Leaving him a manageable list, including tiling both bathroom floors, I said I'd phone for daily updates. And since there would be purchases, I even left him my Home Depot credit card. (You can see where this is headed….)

During my absence, Dave reported that all was quiet, just he and one other guy were crankin' at the property.

But upon my return, I spied charges on my credit card, totaling about $200, for unexplained materials. Calling it to Dave's attention, he casually replied that he'd used my card as a convenience to buy things for another job of his and I should simply subtract the money from his next paycheck.

"But Dave, you didn't ask me. Nor even inform me you'd done it!"

Red flag number ~~4, 5,~~ 6 was up the pole. And I was left wondering if, over the holidays, Dave had really even been at my job every day….

Also, in my absence, he had come up with a bright idea that he pitched over the phone. "Let's flip houses together. You do the designing and I'll do the work." In this fantasy, after completing my house, we two would power on as a design team. Nothing could stop us.

"Only two flaws in that concept," I had to enlighten him, "neither of us has any money to buy another house, and I don't want another ulcer."

"Well, think about it because it's a good idea."

"I don't have to think about it because I don't want to do it."

"Why? You're good at it."

"First of all, that's debatable. Second, in case you haven't noticed, I don't enjoy this work."

Dave was dismayed by my flat refusal. But there were actually three flaws…he was making me nervous. He was now throwing off the rhythm at the job-site by not going home at 5:00 when everyone else wrapped up, but working well into the night instead (when I needed to go study at the Depot).

Also, it's ill-advised to operate power tools a) at night, and b) under fatigue. So I tried hard to discourage Dave's overtime. To no avail. So I just took him as a workaholic bent on making money. But then, while working alone at night at the property, he'd cut himself or drop something on his foot, and next thing I knew, he was seeing his doctor or even at the ER!

That Dave saw his doctor so regularly, like weekly, should've been flag number 7, because that's what drug-dependent people do. But I merely tagged him as accident prone.

Then came our next blindside: the roof issue.

It turned out, the back unit roof, twenty years newer than the front, had been improperly conjoined, creating flooding where the two roofs met. In addition to a pooling situation, where moss and exotic herbs were flourishing, the rainfall overflow down the side of the house had rotted out a portion of that exterior wall.

Water damage, I now know, is far-reaching, insidious, and needs to be dealt with asap. It's also simple to spot, and any legitimate inspector would've highlighted this unchecked disaster, in red, to a potential buyer.

Not Frank.

But since the roof had been *built* wrong, our issue was complex. Reconfiguring it could only be engineered by a master roofer working hand-in-hand with a skilled carpenter.

This was major, and I'd have to scare up more scratch.

Though I'd managed to get an equity loan against my first house, that chunk o' change got devoured like ripe cherries and we were still nowhere close to done. Plus you have to start repaying those loans the second they fund you. So even though I could meet payroll and keep buying materials, I had one more fat monthly bill. And since I'd decided from the start that, when buying a *second house*, one has no business pleading for assistance from relations or friends, and since I had no jewelry to pawn, my only avenue for eking out more dough would be to obtain a home equity loan against this second house.

Some sleuthing revealed that home equity lines of credit (HELOCS) at that lax moment in history were generally being granted without an actual inspection of the property. Banks were simply doing drive-bys to verify that a) the house existed, and b) it appeared worth what the owner had claimed. In my case—with the exterior now painted and all new windows in—the curb appeal was deceivingly sleek. So, believing it could pass muster, I dressed it up for the drive-by, scheduled for Valentine's Day, with sarongs as curtains and attractive potted plants on the front porch. The bank needn't know chaos reigned within.

For this critical event—for which no time was given, just the day—I'd have to evacuate my crew, along with their vehicles, equipment, and noise. But the guys wanted to work and insisted they could do so on the down low. Even when I explained that not getting funding would affect everyone, they insisted on continuing to work. (Their lack of empathy surprised me). Only Homer grasped that, with thousands and thousands at stake, the drive-by inspector needed to believe the work was *completed.*

Again, I had to put my foot down. Each of the workers was given a homemade valentine with a $50 check inside, but forbidden to work. That was the best I could do. No one thanked me, but they did take the day off. And I got a $100,000 loan, so we could finish the job.

Later on, after completing the renovation, when I got back to my own life, stopped eating fast food, and no longer had to salute construction workers at dawn, my ulcer took leave as unexpectedly as it had arrived.

7

The Guys

Ahh, the Andrews, the Daves, the dancers, the delinquents. I wish I could say the following profiles were embellishments:

Dave

I guess one man's Gestapo task-master is another man's dazzling dominatrix, because Dave always let me know that whatever glory I still possessed wasn't lost on him. I made it clear, however, that our job-site was no place for innuendo.

Also from the start, Dave had tall tales about his life experiences: sniper in Afghanistan, undercover CIA operative in Latin America, mercenary in subtropical Africa…and other super-sized assignments no one would've linked him with. At fifty-two, it wasn't implausible to have pulled off a few escapades…but all of them? And banging nails on Kaua'i didn't quite jive as a follow-up. But Dave would toss these high-profile missions into conversations as if mentioning where he ate last night. And when drilled down, he'd just shrug, "Don't believe me, I don't care. Why would I lie?" True, these shores were where both heroes and zeroes washed up. But…questions were dancing around Dave.

Undaunted by them, he remained tireless, reliable, and industrious. With his Midwestern grin, Virgo-clean white t-shirts and khaki shorts, he performed stupendously. And I needed him.

But just a few weeks in, Homer and I noted that Dave had other strange ticks. We'd find penciled scrawl, vaguely profane, on a wooden door frame or piece of drywall, clearly authored by Dave. This random graffiti, apparently intended for no one in particular, was off-color and mildly angry. And soon a couple of other workers commented, "Someone's writing weird things in weird places."

"That's Dave," I told them. "We think he might have some issues."

So I asked Dave about the memos.

"It'll all be painted over anyway," he quipped, "it doesn't matter."

So I let it be…. He was a Godsend in so many capacities.

But the potty-mouth scribble continued raising eyebrows. And whomever the target, it was missing its mark. "Hey Dave," I addressed it again, "what's the purpose of the little notes everywhere?"

"They'll get covered over, it's no big deal."

"Yeah, but they're weird."

"Don't worry about it. They're gonna get covered over."

"I'm not worried, but I'd prefer you don't do it."

"Why does it matter?"

"The other guys don't like it. They find it distasteful and the language offensive…and I have to agree."

"It doesn't have anything to do with anyone—they're just little pencil marks."

"I understand. But better if you don't do it anymore."

He pouted as if losing a privilege. And there may have been a final entry or two, but the naughty notes subsided.

Looking back, Dave was probably a tomcat spraying his territory…judging by the overt disapproval from the other guys. But Homer and I suspected Dave's dormant psychology might shoot him in the foot one of these days.

But I still trusted and even liked the good-natured powerhouse, for whom no job was too big. He even phoned me every morning at 6 a.m. to say, "Good morning, dear." And his workmanship was unsurpassed. I don't know how I'd have managed that remodel without him. So his importance to the operation lent him a certain authority. Plus he owned the marvelous Rosie—though perhaps only to dissuade anyone from sniffing around the back of his pickup looking for drugs.

But about a month into the job, I noticed Dave sometimes getting harsh with Rosie for no reason. I'd intervene, telling him not to be so rough, then I'd give her a hug. But one day, to my horror, he kicked Rosie in the face…for nothing! Like maybe she was in his way when he walked past!

I grabbed and held her. Seething at Dave, I said, "Don't you EVER do that, or anything close to that, to this dog again, or to any animal. Don't you ever, EVER hurt this dog or any other animal ever again!!"

I now knew for sure that something was off with Dave. And I also understood that growly tendency of Rosie's.

Homer

A skinny, mildly emphysemic, Wyoming man in his late sixties, Homer was a philosopher, cigarette smoker, loner, and misogynist. "Women have their place," he'd say, "but no one's figured out yet where it is," or, "There should be a limit to how far lycra can stretch." He never ate or even drank water ("fish pee in it") all day long, and did everything but ride a horse to underscore his Western identity.

But despite being a workaholic, Homer would readily rest his tools, lean against the house in the shade, light a cig, and shoot the breeze with me. He was one of the rare few workers, in all my homeowner years, who totally enjoyed a nice, cynical, gossip break. Probably an excuse to smoke.

Homer was a mushy, simpatico Pisces with a golden heart and artistic bent. I considered him a friend. When we'd encounter some mammoth issue, he'd roll up his sleeves and never let me down. "It's not the end of the world," he'd say, "but you can see it from here."

Emotional fish don't play tough guy too well, though, and Homer was lousy at reprimanding tenants (later on, as my surrogate when I was off island) or delivering them bad news or certified letters. Half the time, the softie would end up siding with the tenants. "They said they're definitely going to pay the rent on Wednesday, and I think they will." Or, "The wife's been sick, they said, so I told them I'd explain that to you."

"Homer, you weren't supposed to negotiate with them, just hand them the letter."

"Well, they seem pretty nice, so I didn't want to be unreasonable."

"Homer, their rent is three weeks late and they've been dodging my calls. They've had plenty of notice that I'd be taking action."

He could even get a bit girlie when nearing his breaking point. On one occasion, eight or ten weeks into the renovation, when all of us (including Rosie, tied to the clothesline) were in the back yard painting and hammering, Homer threw a hissy fit. "I'm done! I'm off this job!" And to everyone's surprise, he marched off the property without a backward glance.

Having given no hint he was at the end of his tether, I could only guess his authority had been undermined by Dave. So I left him a message at the end of the day, "I'm disturbed that you're gone and I'm really sorry for whatever caused it. I just want you to know that if and when you want to come back, immediately or any other time, you're always welcome. And of course I have your check."

But I didn't hear back.

I now know that construction guys, even when committed to a job, are always lining up the next opportunity. Especially toward the end of a stint, juggling more than one gig is commonplace, while not letting on to either employer that they're dividing their time and energy. Sometimes they'll even make it seem like you "forced" them off the job or mistreated them, so they're not accused of jumping ship.

At least my project was under control and I could spare Homer at that point; he didn't leave me in the lurch.

But, lo, a month later—again, we were out toiling in the hot sun—Homer sauntered back in as though he'd just gone for coffee. "I'm back."

"Great!" came the chorus. Though a wishy-washy fishy, everyone knew Homer's commitment and durability out-shined us all. Expressionless, he picked up a paint brush and got back to work.

And a few years later, Homer stunned me when he became not just one of my yoga students, but my best one! He turned out to be, deep down, something of a closet Buddhist, taking to yoga as if he'd been waiting for it all his life.

Eric

There's a sequence to renovation and remodeling. For example, you don't do the ceilings last, because ceiling work can drip all over your floors and walls. So ceilings are done early. And it goes without saying that structural issues are dealt with before the cosmetic side. So if you have to re-wire the electricity, cutting into walls here and there or putting in new sockets, you'll do this before painting.

Early on, I found an electrician named Eric who came over to give an estimate. Another Mainlander, he was thirty-ish, slight, and struck me as educated. Without doing a hard sell to get the job, nor driving a truck, he was well-versed in his subject and seemed competent. Why else would he be looking for electrician work? So I hired him and he began the following day.

Working quietly and efficiently, Eric kept to himself. I'd check in periodically, and things were going smoothly. But I felt a sort of…hesitancy from him.

"How's it going?" I asked at the end of the second day.

"Well…I…."

"What?"

"I, I'm just not sure I want to…do this."

"What do you mean? Is something wrong? It looks like you have a good handle on the situation."

"No, the work's okay…. I-I'm just not sure I want to *do* this…." A faraway look crept into his eye. "Do you mind if I just think it over, maybe overnight? I think I need to reflect on some things."

Not what you'd expect from an electrician, but I said, "Well, it seems like you sort of have to—I can't expect you to do something you don't want to do. So, sure, do whatever you have to do."

He seemed grateful for my response.

"I hope it doesn't take too long," I added.

"No, it won't."

"Okay, just communicate with me as to what happens," I said, as he packed up his stuff.

Next day, late morning, Eric phoned.

"Oh, hi. How are you?" I started.

"I'm good, I'm really good," he sounded more grounded. "I climbed up Sleeping Giant Mountain last night and spent the whole night up there. I gave this whole issue a lot of thought…and I've made up my mind."

"You figured it out?"

"Yes."

"Oh, that's good. That's great. What did you come up with?"

"Yeah, it is great," he said, doubt gone from his voice. "I'm not gonna be— I've realized that…I really don't want to be an electrician."

"You don't?"

"No. I thought about it deeply."

"Oh, well…that's a big realization. Not too good for me, but probably good for you."

"Yeah. I'm sorry to have to tell you."

"Do you know what you're gonna do instead?"

"Yes. I do."
"What's it going to be?"
"I want to be a ballerina."
"A ballerina?"
"Yes."

Not much one can say to that. He didn't say a "ballet dancer," mind you, but "ballerina." I had to let him get on with it.

Anaha

Rob, who later renamed himself Anaha (Hawaiian for "lion"), came across as a normal construction guy from Michigan. And to this day he really is, in fact, that. But temperament is a whole 'nother animal.

I had known Rob before I bought my rental property, so was pleased he was able to join my team. And as one of the initial recruits, I had him do all the ceilings in the three-bedroom front unit. Confident with that, he got busy up on a ladder as Dave and others took on the demolition and preparatory structural stuff in back.

But as Rob began spackling his way across the ceiling, right from the start blobs of plaster were hitting the floor. And especially in the hall and living room, other workers were scuffling through, tracking that fast-hardening white goop throughout the house. After a day or two, I said, "Hey, Rob, would you mind putting drop cloths under where you're working? I'll happily give you some."

He claimed he wasn't making that much of a mess, and what else would I expect when ceilings are being spackled and painted? When I pointed out the splatters everywhere and footprints through them, he replied that none of that mattered because the floors were going to be redone anyway.

"True, but we don't need extra mess around here. The plaster on everyone's shoes ends up all over the house. And I have to clean it up."

"You don't have to clean it up, that's my point. But if you want to make it a problem, that's up to you."

Hmm.

So I let it slide.

LESSON : Male construction workers may really bristle when you a) suggest different practices than they're used to doing, i.e. using a drop cloth, or b) do anything but praise them.

But after another day or two, with plaster all over the house, creating constant mop-up for me and overshadowing Rob's contribution, I decided he was simply wrong, and being contrary for no good reason. "I'm really sorry, Rob," I approached him again, "but I really need you to use drop cloths."

He answered curtly that he knew what he was doing and had never before been told how to do his job.

Dumbfounded at the resistance to a) common sense, b) something so minor, and c) a repeated request from his employer, I just stood there speechless.

Rob then said squarely that he'd finish the job by tomorrow but wouldn't be doing any more work for me.

To that, I just said okay.

He finished the following day, received his check, and split.

After final completion of my renovation, I'd regularly see Anaha at the health food store and cafes. He remained standoffish. It was unfortunate how things had turned out, considering we'd been friendly before the renovation. And with the passing of several years and several sets of tenants, I observed that I'd never had any problems at all regarding my ceilings; in fact, Rob had done a superb job. So one day, I plopped down beside him at an outdoor table at the health food store. "I just wanted to tell you," I said, "that, despite the way things ended with us, you did a great job and I appreciate it. So many things about that project caused me grief, but to this day whenever I look up at the ceilings, they always look great."

He was relieved to let it all go. We resumed our friendship and I hired him again for handyman jobs for the next ten years! Anaha, too, once we buried the hatchet, was a worker who enjoyed a shady gossip break and a chuckle.

Johnny

We were about three months in when I found Johnny, a master carpenter, for the finish carpentry work. ("Finish carpentry," for those who may not know, is the more detailed woodwork—cabinetry, shelving, smaller details, furniture-making.)

In his Bermuda shorts and Panama hat, Johnny was a welcome, if not handsome, addition to my gang. He was a strong, fit, black guy with a ready Texas smile, who knew everything there was to know about his craft. Since his father, too, was a carpenter (always a good sign), woodworking was

Johnny's language, and the longer I knew him, the more his abilities floored me.

Johnny had a model work ethic. He'd arrive *early* each day, pick a shady spot outside well out of everyone's way, then erect a portable table on foldable saw horses, placing a drop cloth beneath them. Attaching his extension cords, he'd then power through his day in a self-sufficient orbit. He'd take precisely thirty minutes for lunch, eating food from home under a tree, then go straight back to work. At 5:00 on the dot, he'd pack everything into his truck, leaving no trace of debris. And he never charged me for his set-up or break-down time. Johnny had more respect for the workplace than any worker I ever hired before or after him. He showed me that being clean, conscientious, and organized was possible in a construction worker.

And his presence on the job, because he was so straight up, proved a turning point in my project. By then, I'd reached my quota of personality disorders, but hadn't yet seen the light at the end of the tunnel. And I remember Johnny's first day, up on the roof with the roofer I hired. From up there, we three could see all Kaua'i's majesty—mountains, ocean, the entire sky. And suddenly, a full rainbow arched right over us, across the whole sky...and just stayed and stayed.

That was my first sign that everything was going to be alright.

Andrew

With a long red ponytail, this lanky, extra tall hippie was adorned in flowy white shirts and gauzy white pants—underwear unimportant. Andrew, who I also met at the health food store, made it readily clear that he sought a lover and I qualified (homeowner). He even weaseled his way over to where I lived, when I mentioned my mango tree was in season. I later learned that, despite a certain insightfulness, he was a card-carrying vagabond, adept at scrounging and surviving off the land. Though claiming he could do everything, he actually could not…aside from sniffing out ripe avocados (or mangos) to pick then sell. And, though competence on the bamboo flute rarely spills over to construction work, Andrew still needed enough paid work to gas up his van. And since I currently needed assistance on every possible front, even nominal chores, I agreed to let him help with some painting.

To assume Andrew was high, on at least pot, might've explained certain telltale characteristics—he was a tad touchy and hypersensitive. But this was back when people weren't necessarily "on something" and daytime was for getting things done. (Now "What are they on?" is a fair question for just about anyone.) So I just left him to his messy, substandard work…for about a week. Until everyone on the job concurred it was senseless paying anyone for that performance level, especially someone dressed for moon dancing. I told Andrew I'd have to let him go.

Oooooh, fatal.

He didn't like being shown the door—went postal, in fact. How dare I question his skillset? He grew so livid that he picked up an ax and began hacking the bathroom where he was previously ~~making a mess~~ painting the baseboards.

As chopping sounds reverberated from the bathroom, and I was shouting, "Stop! Stop! Andrew, stop!" Homer, Dave, and Johnny stood frozen beside me in a row. "Somebody do something! Stop him!" I pleaded to the three brutes beside me, who remained ~~terrified~~ curiously immobile.

It was actually Homer, pushing seventy, who finally stepped up and disappeared into the bathroom where Hippie Andrew was staging his protest. Moments later, the two emerged, Homer talking Andrew down while gently steering him out the front door before he murdered someone. In the background, Johnny, Dave, and I stared from our wide-eyed line, me shaking and praying Homer could insert some calm into the moment, while there was still some house left.

But moments later, Andrew waltzed back in, now holding as hostage my camera that I'd left outside. Accusing me of unfairness, he demanded his pay on the spot.

But Homer the Hero, entering behind him, stepped up again, "Andrew, you're being a little unreasonable right now. Just give me the camera."

Homer's avuncular demeanor was able to pacify Andrew enough to get us all through the ordeal…. Truth was, Andrew revered the kindly older gentleman because Homer could be counted on for the handyman lessons Andrew sorely needed. Whenever Andrew managed to land a job, he'd phone Homer for not just instruction but to borrow tools for the task. It's not known what Homer got in return.

Shortly after terrorizing the whole house, leaving hack marks on the baseboards and his painting paraphernalia akimbo, Andrew left in a huff. With group relief, we four shook it off as best we could, while I profusely thanked Homer. But I was never to comprehend why Johnny (young and fit) and Dave (a bison) left rickety Homer to subdue the ax man.

Though I told Andrew that he'd be paid on Friday with everyone else, that evening, a Wednesday, he phoned me at home. (This was back when answering machines allowed you to listen in as callers left messages.) "I want my money!" he demanded. "And I'm coming to get it right now!" He knew where I lived and was on his way…still furious!

Since only hours earlier, this tree-hugger had hacked up my baseboards, I didn't relish another confrontation, especially alone. But having no allies on Kaua'i to call, I breathlessly phoned Johnny, who'd only been on the job a few days. "Andrew just left me a message saying he's coming here right now and he wants his money!"

"Get in your car and come straight to my house. Get in your car *immediately* and come straight over here." Johnny hastily gave directions.

Having no idea how close Andrew was, I grabbed my cat and flew out the door without even flip-flops.

Johnny, it turned out, was house-sitting a glamorous North Shore estate. So when I arrived, disheveled, cat-in-hand, he offered me a bedroom suite and insisted I stay the night. Thus began a solid friendship with Johnny that lasted years. And I hired him many more times.

Andrew got his check when he showed up at the job-site Friday, while everyone stood by, braced for action. But like most drug addicts, he just needed the money.

Small island life being what it is, I saw Andrew around town a lot after that. And after an awkward year or two, to my surprise, he sincerely apologized one day. So I accepted it. Then he received an inheritance and wafted to other shores.

Millard

Further into the renovation came Millard, a black, bean-pole plumber from Baltimore. At least six-five and probably the only qualified plumber able to slither under the back unit of that house—that was built too low to the ground—Millard, too, did brilliant work. And his assignments were no joke. He's the one who moved the toilet across the bathroom, as well as re-plumbed the whole back unit to accommodate that new kitchen, featuring sink-in-middle-of-room, built into an L-shaped counter (my ~~indulgent~~ brilliant design).

Millard was around for at least a month and, after about three weeks, Homer figured out he was quite the Casanova.

On small islands, people know people who know people. And it turned out, more than one middle-aged lady around town was in love with Millard, while others had been. Fortunately for my project, Millard never flirted with me (I was too sober and straight). Homer also linked Millard's skinniness and ongoing lack of money, despite steady income, to probable drug use. But although never showing up until 10 or 11, Millard was dependable and knew his trade. Whatever madcap soirees he was recovering from, the cool cat bore no trace of weariness, laziness, or burnout. And no one on the job ever had a problem with him or his easy manner.

But the true magic of Millard was that he fit under that house.

Vern

After Twinkle Toes twirled away, I had to go pro on the electricity. So I went to the Yellow Pages to find someone established enough to pay for advertising.

And Vern was a find. His thing was to spend half the year doing electricity on Kaua'i and the other half on a fishing boat in Alaska. He was making tons of money, even had properties and was a landlord. It was he, actually, who passed along a valuable landlord tip that I followed for the next sixteen years. *LESSON :* Keep the utility bills in your name to simplify things and even to make a little extra money.

When Vern first appeared to give an estimate, he was so concise about what we'd need, how long it would take, and exactly what he'd accomplish, he convinced me on the spot to hire him. His approach was, "Yes, it's gonna cost you to hire me, but you're gonna get the best possible job. I know what I'm doing and I work fast—I'm a wham-bam kind of guy. I'll be at your house for two nonstop work days. I'll have two other guys with me, we'll put in everything you need, and you'll never look back." He also wanted a flat rate, "What I quote you will be your total cost—no extras, no surprises afterwards." Vern's only caveat was, "But while I'm working, I'll be going insane throughout the whole house, so all your other workers have to step back and let me do my thing. I need free rein of the place. But when I'm done, your house is gonna be wired up with everything you could ever need, you're gonna be happy, you're gonna give me my check, then you'll never see me again."

I signed him on. His agenda unfolded seamlessly, he didn't even pause for breath. And I held up my end by telling all the other workers, "For the next two days, whatever Vern wants, Vern gets. You have to stay out of his way completely so he and his guys have full access to everything electrical.

You can coordinate with them, but Vern's top dog for these two days." I even gave a couple of guys time off.

Almost overnight, the electricity was re-wired throughout the house with bells and whistles. I gratefully handed Vern the amount he'd quoted me, and I never looked back. In all the years to follow, I never had an electrical issue. And I never did see Vern again.

Mine was not an atypical tropical island work brigade. But I never forgot my LA friend's warning, "When people leave all their troubles behind and go start over on some remote island, Hawai'i's where they go." After just these few months, I'd already found that 75% of the guys working this housing boom had substance issues, credibility issues, skill issues, honesty issues, penitentiary issues, identity issues, or many of the above. And what they'd left on the Mainland included abandoned offspring and child support, and one or more recent wives or lovers. Johnny had six-year-old twins in Chicago. Homer had a daughter in her twenties in Georgia. Millard had three kids in Baltimore. And Dave…well…who knew?

Just an Aside

An aside pertaining to male workers and any fantasy they may entertain about their female boss….

Well, I wasn't *opposed* to a relationship, particularly with a handy guy with looks, muscles, and an honest profession. But call me old school, if someone wants to be my lover, ask me out. For instance, after many months in my employ, Rudy, my awesome gardener on that job, who at the end was leaving for the Mainland, said, "Too bad you and me never got together. All you had to do was wink."

Wink? I don't wink at workers. Or anyone over age ten or under age ninety. Plus Rudy, it turned out, lived in a tent, and consumed undisclosed quantities of beer in there every night.

One or two others of my workers might've had boy-friend appeal in certain lighting, and seemed open to the prospect. But in the Book of Etiquette, isn't it a no-no to romance people you're paying by the hour? I mean, if the guy can't take you to dinner or a movie (or both, heaven forbid)…and if they don't own a house, and you own two…?

I did learn, in owning two properties as a single woman, that men without property were especially keen on being my soulmate.

I mean, sometimes I'd invite a worker to dinner if, say, we'd just completed a big task or we needed to discuss something about the job, or even if we just needed to relax after working hard. But they always let me pick up the tab. I had intended to, of course, but month after month, they never offered *anything,* even while remaining "interested." Couldn't they see how much I could benefit from a competent male in my life? Or notice that I knew almost no one on the island? Had they offered help in the smallest way, or ever once uttered, "Hey, you don't have to pay me for that Home Depot run," or "I'll get dinner this time," they might've won me. But they didn't. I hate to generalize, but I'm not sure this industry boasts the most gallant of men.

8

Caution: Men at Work

Ruffling Feathers

Macho men, construction workers in particular, aren't as creative as you'd expect or wish. Despite their physical advantages, attitudes, and blanket refusal to admit when they don't know, they actually prefer being told what to do, and to then just go do it. They won't do the thinking for you because a) they're not hired to, b) they truly don't know your vision, and c) they don't dare steer you wrong because they don't want the blame. Their mission is to a) make money, and b) hopefully please you by doing a good job. It's quite simple …but hard for a woman to figure out. Because, unlike us, they don't fancy discussing it more than the bare minimum. They'd rather be told not nearly enough, then pester you later with petty questions ("Where's the sponge?") than have things spelled out beforehand ("Here's your sponge"). They want to throw themselves into the project, do decent work in order to stay on this gig a little longer or maybe get hired by you again someday, and make as much money as possible. They're counting down the hours until 5:00 when they can crack open their brewski. They want to satisfy you but, for reasons mysterious to the fair sex, can't bear confabulating about how the job should or will unfold. They don't get, and never will, why it's useful to chart out where we're going and to be in sync with their employer.

"I got this, lady," is what they project. Then later, "Oh, did you say you have a drop cloth somewhere?" And later still, "Yeah, and I'm gonna need some number 200 sandpaper."

"Oh. When will you need it?"

"Now."

"Great, I just got back from the Home Depot."

And did I mention that you're their step-and-fetch-it for the duration, as well as scullery maid?

So you walk on eggshells around them. If you need to ask a question or, God forbid, *change something* while guys are working, cross yourself, put on kid gloves, and approach on tiptoe. Bowing at their feet doesn't hurt. Because aside from the communicative or easygoing few, these men abhor being questioned or "supervised" by someone like *you*—you don't even have a truck. Plus they're over tired and drugged on junk food, thus testy about any benign phrase or word that could even vaguely be interpreted as questioning their skill or integrity. Like, should you press for information, change your concept, or make suggestions *while they're working*, you're asking for it. And should they throw a certain steely glance your way, they're a breath away from marching off the job, never to return. "Find somebody else, I'm done." Happened to me several times.

LESSON : Spell out your job expectations before and during a guy's employ.

In all fairness, though, I did learn that just because someone appears to be simply hammering nails into a piece of wood, or sawing a length of quarter-round in two, carpentry and building involve real calculus. What may appear mindless labor regularly requires organizing, sequencing, thought, focus, and precision.

On the other hand, *you're* the boss, and if you're too acquiescent, you'll soon be working for them, while paying for the privilege.

Through the construction phase, I learned new angles on how different men and women are. Mainly, that men handle intensity differently than women. Men feel responsible for it in a way women really don't. Call me politically incorrect, but watch what happens when there's a flat tire, or a couch has to be moved out of a truck, or a heavy suitcase has to go into the overhead bin. Or even if the cat's stuck in a tree.

Because my crew felt "responsible" for all that needed to get done, a certain edginess could prevail. Like any time something went even slightly wrong—perhaps I'd innocently ask, "What's that? What's going on there?"—they'd stand accused, as if I was on their case. But I had the female perspective, "I want to figure this out. Let's analyze the situation." Their educated opinion could be as valuable as their energy output, especially regarding momentous or costly choices.

Men weren't on that page. Paid by the hour, their thinking was, "Do you really want me to chat with you right now? Shouldn't I get back to work?" So they'd retort, "That was so-and-so who did that work. What do you want ME to do about it? Just say what you want done now."

Having been taught by the rafter tails that a) different workers are familiar with different things, b) all the ultimate cost and responsibility would be mine anyway, and c) a giant mistake would set me back way more than a fifteen minute chat at $25/hour, it was imperative I harvest as much advance intel as possible. So my feeling was always, "We're doing what we have to do in this moment—I *don't know* exactly where we're going from here, I'm trying to get more perspective! So let's talk through it."

But you have to cultivate an attitude that doesn't intimidate macho workers.

LESSON : One suggestion might be to say at the beginning of their employment, "There may be times when I'll need to discuss construction details with you, or ask your advice about how to proceed with something, or just need to brainstorm with you about some aspect of the project. If I ask for your attention just to talk, you'll still be on the clock, don't worry."

Also, decision making crops up frequently during construction projects. And numerous are the laborers who'll either guess what you'd prefer or proceed according to their own preference. But women want things the way they want things. Don't ask why. And married men learn not to debate them. But plenty of rogue singles populate this industry, and being more experienced than you is their justification for making unilateral decisions when questions arise.

To avoid finding work done differently than you requested, it's best to tell workers from the start, "If you have any questions or hesitancy about what's next or what you're supposed to do, ask me, ask me, ask me." When I had to leave the job-site, my parting words were always, "Call me for any reason. I'd much rather you ask me than guess or make a decision on your own about how it should go." But even after overstating it like that, they'd still wing it! And rarely ask questions.

So if I wanted things to go as I thought we had discussed, a critical part of my job was vigilance. Without micro-managing (the female micro-manager is a construction worker's vampire), I had to keep an eagle eye on *everything*.

LESSON : It's worth stating to your workers, "I don't want to pay you to do it, pay you to undo it, then pay you to redo it."

An artful tactic some construction workers pull is to fudge their assignment when you're not around. Then when you return and find the work done differently than requested, they simply say, "Oh, I thought you said bla-bla-bla."

"Really?? That's not what I said," you're gobsmacked.

For example, my back porch had some 4-by-4 posts holding up the overhang. At the top of each post, bracing the 4-by-4, were two 2-by-4 supports at forty-five degree angles. And though there was *nothing wrong with those 2-by-4 supports*, I wanted to change them to 4-by-4's for a sturdier look. Strictly for aesthetics, because these posts could be seen through the kitchen window, and even as you entered the front door. And since Dave could knock this out blindfolded, it seemed an easy upgrade.

But construction workers get antsy about unnecessary application. Why would a woman under duress spend time and money on an architectural flight of fancy? "She must be secretly loaded."

Naive to tactics, I put Dave on that job and headed off to the Depot or one of my other haunts.

Returning an hour later, I saw the 2-by-4's had been replaced by new 2-by-4's, instead of 4-by-4's, as instructed. "Dave, why did you put more 2-by-4's in there?"

"I thought that's what you said."

"Why would I replace perfectly good 2-by-4's with new 2-by-4's? The point was to *remove* the 2-by-4's. I said to put in **4-by-4's.**"

"Oh," casual as pie, even dismissive, "I thought you said 2-by-4's. I thought you wanted those out because they were older and you wanted new ones."

"That's not what I wanted, and I was very clear about it." Huge sigh, while shaking my head in disbelief. "Could you please now put in 4-by-4's?"

"Okay, sure. I'll do it right now. Won't take long."

Dave heard me fine. If not, he would've asked, "Why are you replacing perfectly good 2-by-4's with new 2-by-4's?" But "mistakes" equal more hours' pay, and Dave spotted a couple of hours' extra money because I was off at the Depot. Later on, I learned that this is one of the tricks of the trade.

So if you turn your back and leave workers to it, you risk them screwing up, but if you watch them like a hawk, you're micro-managing. *LESSON :* Be really clear about what you ask workers to do, especially if you won't be overseeing them. Because once they've done it wrong, you're stuck.

You'll never hear, "I'm sorry. I messed up. I'll redo it at no charge." What you will hear is, "That's not what you said. You didn't say to do that.'"

"Yes, I did."

"Well, I didn't hear you say that."

Arguing is futile. As is insisting he did hear you, then not paying him for that work. And you can't fire him, because you need him. All you can do is let it go. But whether mishaps or ploys, these discrepancies occur and you take the hit.

Also fairly early on, Homer matter-of-factly said, "You do realize, don't you, that every time you leave, everybody stops working?"

"No, I didn't realize."

LESSON: It's good to make lists itemizing what you need guys to do. Include details. Having things written on paper a) proves what you said, so there's no opening for misunderstanding; b) means they don't have to remember everything you mentioned and can just churn down the list; and c) assuages their fears that the wild woman will throw some new curve when they're halfway through an assignment.

When a number of tasks need to be done, guys actually prefer having a list.

9

The Gal

Then one day, Johnny mentioned that Dave had offered him morphine. And it all came together—the overdrive, the bad-boy graffiti, the need to make enough money to pay for his drugs, the not eating, the doctor-as-significant-other, the overkill approach to assignments, the credit card episode, the general nonconformance, even the mistreatment of Rosie (just a guard dog).

With Johnny's news flash, I needed to get Dave off the job. Things wouldn't be bettering. So in hopes that he'd quit, I told him I could only pay him $25 an hour going forward, not $35. With real estate still booming on Kaua'i and construction work abundant, I expected the salary cut would send him packing. But Dave opted to stay and just resent me. And, to still earn enough for his morphine or whatever, he started cheating on his hours, taking more side jobs, and telling more lies. And when I wasn't on hand, he'd pretend to be at the job when he wasn't, collecting double pay whenever possible.

Johnny then informed me that every time I walked out the door, Dave left minutes later. And when I'd return and phone Dave, he'd just say, "Oh I'm around the corner, I went to 7-Eleven for a soda. Be right back!"

His house of cards was crumbling. He wasn't even up to date on the rent where he lived, in a house he'd claimed to own. With tension mounting and Dave fraying, finally I said, "If you tell me one more lie, Dave, we're done."

Within thirty minutes he lied again about hours worked or jobs completed or something else. "We're done," said I.

I never mentioned that I knew about the morphine, but his kicking Rosie in the face still spooked me.

Things grew even worse for the guy. After our farewell, I heard he'd finagled my sweet, elderly, next-door neighbors into painting part of their home's exterior. Having observed him working at my house twelve hours a day for months, they considered him solid. But after extracting a $200 deposit from them, Dave never did the work. Then Johnny got word that Dave had taken a $5000 deposit from someone on the North Shore and hadn't honored that commitment either.

That's when, maybe a week later, Andrew the Ax Man, of all people, showed up at my rental to report that, with everyone after him, Dave was suddenly gone—run off the island. And when he fled, he left Rosie tied to a pole in front of the house he didn't own. Andrew said Rosie had initially been adopted by a neighbor but had soon escaped and was now at large. And her adoptive home didn't want her back because of that growly thing.

Andrew spilled these bad beans into my lap, knowing I was the only member of Rosie's fan club who might do something. Certainly, no one else in Dave's small circle was in a position to care for a dog, or even had the time to find her.

So I thanked Andrew, then immediately phoned the Humane Society. "We have no dog of that description," the man said. "But you should come in anyway to look for her."

"Why would I come in when you just told me she's not there?"

"You should come in to check anyway.... But we're closing right now, so come tomorrow."

Confused by the double-speak, I'd go in next morning anyway. And that evening, I scoured Dave's neighborhood, speaking to everyone I encountered, but there were no leads as to Rosie's whereabouts.

The next morning, a staff person at the Humane Society directed me to the dog section to look around. There, I studied the heartbreaking hopefuls, each described by a card clipped to their cell. Halfway down the row of pleading brown eyes, I found an empty cage that, to my astonishment, bore a tag reading, "ROSIE. Medium-sized mixed breed. Friendly, well trained, and extremely obedient. Would make a great family dog."

What?!

Speeding back to the front desk, I told the staffer, "There's a cage that says 'Rosie' on it and it perfectly describes the dog I'm looking for. Can you tell me where she is?" I then held my breath as he perused the database.

"Let me go check something," he said, and stepped away.

Had I found her?

The guy returned, "Are you the owner?"

"I'm the person responsible for her. She doesn't really have an owner anymore. I'm the only one who's gonna show up here. What's going on with her?"

"The dog's been put in quarantine. Only owners are permitted to see dogs in quarantine."

"Quarantine? Why is she in there?"

"She tested positive for Heart Worm. Because of that, she can't be adopted out. Heart Worm's very serious and expensive to treat. And we can't even release her to her owner unless the owner agrees to very costly treatments for the rest of the dog's life."

I stared in disbelief. "Can I see her?"

"Only the owner can see her…."

As I stood flabbergasted, the man's humane side crept in, "But if she doesn't have an owner, I guess we could call you the owner." And with my eager nod, he led me through the clinical, gated maze of barks to a more foreboding block of stainless steel cages. Here in Solitary, the worst of 'em were sequestered.

He opened one of the thick, overly scrubbed doors, and who should we see, jumping ecstatically around after hearing my voice? "She obviously knows you," said the guy, as the jubilant prisoner assumed she was being sprung.

The man left Rosie and I to our reunion, and I assured her everything was going to be alright. Though she seemed surer about it than I. At least she was found, frisky, and fed.

Leaving her momentarily, I returned to the front desk. "What happens now?"

"Well, Heart Worm is serious. The reason we don't release animals with Heart Worm for adoption is because few owners have the kind of money necessary for the treatment costs."

"How much are you talking about?"

"Around $100,000."

"Excuse me, what planet are we on?" I did not say. I just stared. Then I repeated, "*A hundred thousand dollars?*"

"Yeah."

"That's insane."

"Yeah, but that's how much it costs to treat Heart Worm for a number of years. This dog's fairly young and will need the treatment the rest of her life."

"So, what are her options?"

"The only way she can be released is to her owner, and that's only if the owner signs an official affidavit stating he or she has sufficient funds and is willing to pay for Heart Worm medication the rest of the dog's life."

"I'm willing to do that," I said.

His turn to be incredulous, "You're willing to pay $100,000 for the Heart Worm treatment? And you'll sign the paper attesting to that?"

"Yes."

"Okay..." he paused to register this improbable response, "...then we'll call you Rosie's owner...and you can take her."

"Great."

As he went to retrieve Rosie, I mentally affirmed my own truth: "Obviously I don't have $100,000 for this absurdness. But a) clearly, Rosie will be euthanized if I don't rescue her today, b) they'll never track me to check that I followed their prescription, and c) for the first time in my whole adult life, I actually AM in a position to own a dog. I have a house with a big yard, and my rental renovation is nearly finished, so I have time for her. Plus, I've always wanted a dog exactly like Rosie. So the second we march out that door, I'll dismiss the Heart Worm thing and never mention it to a living soul. If Rosie ever shows signs of something wrong, heaven forbid, I'll deal with it then. But right now I'm gonna treat her like a healthy dog. And even if, on some distant date, she dies of Heart Worm, at least she will have had a great life."

There, I was crystal clear.

Rosie bounded out to greet me, and I realized I'd been her owner from the day we met.

I signed the papers, paid the release fee, and we sprang out of there.

I never spent a dime on Heart Worm, never had her tested for it, and it was never mentioned again. And Rosie thrived.

In fact, after about six months of mutual bliss, her growly thing also completely evaporated, never to return.

The combination of moving to the most beautiful place on Earth, then adopting the most incredible dog, was how I got through the next three years, if not six. You can handle a lot of tribulation, uncertainty, loneliness, and risk, if your gratitude is thunderous for what you *do have.* I had Kaua'i, work I enjoyed (massage and yoga), my beautiful first house, a long-term financial plan, and now the winning company of the marvelous Rose to explore the island with. We swam, hiked, dried off in the trade winds, and were the very, very best of friends. For a long, long time. In fact, without Rosie, I don't know how I would've survived that period of my life. I love her forever.

And sometimes when I'm driving, I still reach behind me and slide my hand under the chin of her spirit in the back seat.

So, for all Dave's foibles and the vicissitudes he imposed, especially toward the end, he did great work that still endures …and through him, I got Rosie.

10

Slowly Learning

In the renovation phase, the things people warned me about weren't what plagued me most. I didn't mind that, out here mid-Pacific, we couldn't quickly get supplies. Didn't mind the limitations—from people to hire, to working in the hot sun, to too much rain, to certain supplies and materials not being available *at all*. Didn't mind waiting for the Matson container to float in, nor the minimal choices when it finally docked. All part of the island charm. In fact, if you're seeking ease, convenience, or the latest and the greatest, don't move to the middle of the world's largest ocean.

But what threw me, maybe scarred me for life, were the things I didn't know about or expect:

1. Radically inaccurate estimates for what my renovation costs would be.

2. Structural complications that *no one* knew how to deal with, lastly me. And certain issues requiring construction genius, exhaustive experimentation, or professionalism exceeding my purse.

3. That a crew could fluctuate as continuously as mine did.

4. Idiosyncratic personalities of said crew.

5. The nature of tropical island reality—"Surf's up," an ongoing interruption. Plus the string of opportunists with *soi-dissant* and untraceable credentials who follow construction booms.

6. Overages. Based on guesswork and sketchy advice of near-strangers, the veritable cost of renovating a house just this side of a tear-down is nothing a novice could accurately surmise.

7. There's no backing away once you've begun your remodel. Even if you sense you've made a life-shattering error. With all the windows out, nothing painted, the floor half gone, and trucks all over the lawn, your property has almost no value at this moment. Nobody wants a skeleton of a house. So, all you can do is hang in…and keep spending.

8. Total cost by the time you're done, and facing *decades* to pay it off, or at least down. Also, just managing such unwieldy, unexpected debt. Or else sell the place way sooner than slated and jettison your long-term plan!

9. The reality of landlording. Replacing lightbulbs, refrigerators, and towel racks is the least of it. You can eventually handle these details in your sleep. The grey hairs come from the random and unprecedented curves thrown by tenants, because there are no "normal" ones, just one surprise package after another. I doubt there's a landlord on record who'd dare even whisper, "I've seen it all." No matter how you prep your psyche to not repeat mistakes, bet your toolbox that the one situation you never dreamed of is…on its way.

10. The tricks I didn't know. In any profession, there are best practices and even tricks. Unfortunately, I had no experienced forerunner, or "How Not To" book to brief me on such.

11. Financial game plan. Mine didn't unfold even close to my guesses or projections (except that property values did continue increasing, thank heavens). The weather forecast in the Land of Money is unpredictable. And where there's risk, you can expect fluctuation.

LESSON : With a long-term real estate investment, you must bargain for recessions, interest rate changes, market slumps, pandemics (!), and natural disasters—hurricanes, floods, fires, earthquakes, mudslides, tornados. Not to mention personal or family drama and your own life changes—parents growing old, grandchildren being born, career shifts, divorce, illness, troublemakers in the family, fluke expenses, high school sweethearts on the East Coast wanting you back, inheritances, and the ramifications of living in a remote, unfamiliar locale. At least some of these WILL ambush you, possibly for a number of years.

12. Desperation. There are occasions where you absolutely need new tenants quickly and suitable ones aren't showing up. Maybe the place is empty and you're paying the mortgage, maybe you need to travel to see an ailing parent…. But you can't leave the place empty for any considerable time. So even if not intuitively on board with certain applicants, you may think, "They're clean, they have jobs, and they're paying $100/month more than the last bunch…." while dismissing that inner voice that says, "Something's off here."

But if you take sketchy tenants, sooner or later, you'll pay the piper.

Yet…simple time itself has a way of easing the strain of just about everything. You can actually get used to discomfort, disappointment, inconvenience, and *debt.* Even your hard-knocks perspective can soften, and your knowledge base widen…. You mature. You may even get nicer and more tolerant with tenants, or stricter and less tolerant. I became a little of each. In light of everything, though, I continued believing it could all work out if I could just *stay the course*. And eventually owing less on one's rental property alleviates some pressure. Even tenant issues seem more palatable with financial demands letting up.

When I bought my first Kaua'i house in 2003, my net worth was $195,000. Fourteen years later (despite the seven-year recession), thanks to that rental property, my net worth was $920,000.

Also, one may have countless moments of pride and joy when spending time at the property. I transformed a disaster into the nicest house in the neighborhood, then later upgraded it to even more desirable. And over the years, I resided in both units, twice each, and was snowed by how unexpectedly sweet it was living in that house.

LESSON : Hard work pays off. You have the satisfaction and joy of accomplishing something big. And that changes who you *are*. And hangin' in brings a compounded pay-off, like saving $20 a week until one day you have $10,000.

MAJOR LESSON : Tenacity can really pay off. Long-term rewards CAN be reaped.

"Stay the course," remained my mantra the full sixteen and a half years I owned my rental property. And I chanted it plenty.

Additional Lessons

1. Know your rental neighborhood. Do some research. *LESSON :* Factor in the demographics of where you're buying. Face value is one thing, what the realtor says is another, but your

own intel gathering will help predict what sort of tenants you'll attract, as well as how the neighborhood may evolve with time. My property was in a mixed and changing community, predominantly Filipino. And I knew nothing about that culture. In fact, arriving on Kaua'i, I didn't even know the demographic breakdown of the island. (My overarching concerns in purchasing rental property were affordability, proximity to my other house, and suitable layout.) Though I probably would've proceeded no matter what, understanding the demographics would've spared me discouragement, confusion, and false assumptions about how the neighborhood might transition with time.

2. *LESSON :* Have or make a utility closet at your rental property to keep the supplies/tools you'll regularly need there.

3. With construction workers, you need to run a tight ship, but not too tight. For example, I could've, maybe should've, checked over their invoices more fastidiously, but believed a trusting ambiance was more important than nit-picking or appearing to question their integrity. If they were rounding up to the next hour, I preferred not to know. When you're in thousands upon thousands, this ain't the time to nickel and dime anyone. If a guy was reliable and doing awesome work, I could pay him a little extra.

But glance over invoices for completeness as you receive them, and have a tidy process for handling them. You might need them for tax purposes later; or to refer back to, to review costs or work done; or to reconnect with a certain worker. And your workers then perceive you as professional and diligent.

Too, it's best not to pay workers in cash, so you have records of what you've spent or what certain projects cost you. And pay in full on the day everyone expects to be paid. "I'll pay you the other half next week," will induce latent childhood behavior you'd rather not witness. But don't give them extra, to be nice, when you don't have change or are in a good mood. These gestures are construed as, "She's rich."

LESSON : It behooves you to require legibly printed invoices that include all the data needed for your records. Invoices should be addressed to you, and contain worker's name, business name if applicable, date of invoice, description and date of work performed, number of hours worked at what rate, total amount due, worker's signature, all receipts for materials purchased and paid for by worker, and itemization of all receipts.

4. Don't keep any worker around who, after a trial period, does poor work or continues bothering you in some way. Problematic personalities normally stay problematic, often implying YOU are the problem. *LESSON* : There's always someone else who can do a job and wants work. You just have to find them.

5. Never pay in advance for work uncompleted. Of course, for bigger jobs, like a new roof or full exterior paint job, you must pay at least half up front, plus the cost of materials, so the person can afford to get started and can work in good faith that you have funding. Then the balance is paid upon job's completion. But for guys working by the hour, day, or week, don't pay anything up front. Pay in full at the end of the job, or every week if the work is ongoing.

The reason is psychological: we all work *for money*. It's the reward. Once money's received, the impetus to earn it dissipates. Everything can really slow down after money changes hands. "I'll be back to finish up tomorrow," then he doesn't return for three days. Or you have to chase him up to get that last room painted. He really intended to do it…but you gave him all his money so he's on to the next thing.

6. Get a P.O. box for your address on all correspondence with tenants, including the lease. Tenants needn't know where you live. Even after you've known them a while. Because they can get bees in their bonnets. Some issues blow over, but some don't. Even after vacating, occasional tenants hold grudges. (See Chapter 21, "Harvey the House Husband.") You don't want someone with their boxers in a bunch showing up on your porch. Or doing stealth drive-bys at 11 p.m. (I try hard not to divulge my home address *ever*, so it won't appear on Internet searches. But good luck widdat!)

7. Go by the book. It's close to impossible not to feel insulted, depressed, frustrated, and discombobulated when rascals you barely know are rude, accusatory, discourteous, or attempt to wrangle out of a deal that was agreed to and signed. But it's not you personally that tenants are targeting. Certain low-lifes railroad every landlord they get. And a small percentage even sequentially work the angles.

8. *LESSON :* You'll never get a complete handle on dealing with tenants. Humans have too many variables to be predictable. So don't expect to master that part of the job. Focus on a cool mindset instead, and you'll be less derailed.

A Viable Option

There's always the option of having a property manager handle things for you. S/he will cost you 10-20% of your rent monies every month, but will find the new tenants and communicate with them, collect the rents, and hire the plumbers, electricians, repair people, or whoever's needed in a given situation. A property manager will get your leases signed and be your spokesperson for the property, even take care of evictions. You can be invisible; tenants need never meet you.

LESSON : For many landlords, especially those with multiple properties, and those comfortable with delegating and with paying extra to avoid headaches and life interruptions, a management company is a no-brainer.

But though your stress quotient is minimized, you surrender supervision and sign off on selection and over-sight of both tenants and workers, though still footing the bill for repairs and labor.

I was never hands-off enough to let someone else run the show. But you may be fine with it.

Just understand, property managers are get-the-job-done types, not "Let's explore our options, then screen a few professionals for estimates" types. They a) don't want to screw up, b) are super busy with dozens of units, and c) are spending your money, not their own, when hiring workers, so they rarely shop around for the best deal. They have their go-to list of tradesmen, and may hire more expensive workers than you might. But they may also get better, faster results than you might.

About five years in, reeling from tenant duress, I went to Carter's office—since he was the only other landlord I knew. Fighting back tears, I begged him for advice, "How do you deal with it? I thought this would be a lot easier."

"Tenants are a pain in the ass," he shook his head, "but they're making me rich. That's how I look at it."

With my sky-high debt in those early years, I couldn't yet view tenants as financially valuable. But Carter spoke the truth. No one's a landlord because they're passionate about providing housing.

11

The 'Finish' Side

At long last, we were approaching the creative portion of the program, the cosmetic flourishes I'd once believed were the essence of renovation. With Johnny's panache, the shelving and cabinetry were coming together, complete with bamboo steps built into the upraised living room in the back unit. He even, when I wasn't looking, took the liberty of framing in wood the big vanity mirror in the back bathroom—a Johnny thing no one else would've thought of, and a Johnny flare to quietly do it 'just because.'

For me though, even appetizing activities like selecting lighting fixtures, tiles, or colors for walls were demoted to mere chores on the checklist. With all design decisions governed by limited supply and availability ("We only have three boxes left of that tile"), and what may or may not be on the next barge, design choices were rarely fancy-free. Plus, I was always rushed, because even fun assignments couldn't eclipse my concerns about what might be going down back at the ranch.

Doors

Every single door in that house needed replacing, including exterior ones. And one might speculate, "Just unhinge 'em and pop in new ones." Even plenty of construction guys think hanging doors takes just common sense and basic tools. Friend, hanging doors is an *art form*. Like so much in life and construction, if not performed knowledgeably and with exactitude, it can be maddeningly time consuming and riddled with mishap. (And doors don't fit into a sedan.)

Even before hanging, both sides of the new door need several coats of finish or paint—to be applied whilst door is still on sawhorse—plus drying time between coats. So, with your worker on the clock during drying time, you'll need additional busywork ready for him.

And door frames, those wicked jambs, aren't necessarily perfectly rectangular, nor identical in size to your new hollow-core, "standard door" from the Home Depot. Plus, the doorknob hole on the new door needs to align, to the millimeter, with the old hardware still screwed into your frame. And sometimes it doesn't. Next, with veritable sleight-of-hand, notches for your hinges must be carved into this new door. Then, with precision, this door gets screwed onto those old hinges waiting in the frame. (Though at least half the time you'll need new hinges, because the old ones are rusty or aged, or you're now going brushed nickel and the old ones are gold. Meaning you just hope and pray you can score the same size again.)

But oops, once a door's hung, if it's even the slightest bit off kilter, it will stick, drag, or not properly close. Then you're stuck taking it down again, re-adjusting your hinges, tweaking your notches, sanding down one edge of the door, or even shaving off an edge by some fraction to make it fit into the frame. Great way to destroy a door.

Here's the kicker…once you start sanding edges and messing with the actual shape of your new door, you can sand yourself into a tizzy, only to become unhinged yourself, along with your now useless new door. I've recycled more than one chintzy hollow-core door into a makeshift desk, after too much sanding and moving of hinges rendered them write-offs.

During the remodel, I was blessed to find Tom, a door whiz who hung all my doors in a week. True, he was another Mainland man who'd swapped out a wife and three teenagers in Colorado to become a single surfer in Paradise, but he did great work.

So the bulk of my door tutorials came later, from tenant love quarrels—when doorknob hardware was either forced to the breaking point by someone locked out, or an angry fist proved just how flimsy hollow-cores really are. Practically cardboard.

Note: If you don't mind spending more, and can manage the extra weight of solid doors, or you just want a strong, more classic house, solid wood doors can abide way more abuse than hollow-cores. And considering the hassle and expense of door replacement, solids are a better bet. They're far superior noise buffers, too. But even though they're not that much more expensive, solid wood doors are perceived as a luxury landlords don't touch. (For the above reasons, though, at least consider them.)

After Tom, along came Kelvin and George, a jolly pair of alcoholics with the vibe of banjo players. This paint-and-drywall duo adored working hard as long as they a) could be together, and b) weren't late for their five o'clock froth. They guffawed their way through every room. And I kept them on as long as there were walls to plaster, savoring every minute of the grief they never caused me.

The Paint Paradigm

But let's get down to basics…because *someone* needs to address this: Paint itself is just WEIRD.

What you see on the color charts, and even in the can, is *not* what you get on your wall. And no one can explain why. (Well, one recent paint store worker had a decent take on it, but his explanation was so elaborate and academic that I won't burden you with it.) Paint plays that same tired ruse performed by articles of clothing you buy without trying on—once it's on, you can't believe how wrong it is! "How could this be?"

Aside from becoming deceitfully *darker* once on the wall, you'll find that even the most minuscule differential in paint shade or tint changes the entire mood of a room. That yummy butter-yellow, almost edible in the can, that took you weeks to decide upon for your kitchen, has now turned your breakfast haven into a Mexican restaurant. That drowsy pale peach you painstakingly blended for the guest bedroom looks like the corner strip mall with the pizza place and the dry cleaner.

"What's going on?"

My advice is to choose paint *uncomfortably* lighter than what you think you want. Better still, spend six bucks extra and get a mini color sample to try it out. Otherwise, you're all but promised to be super bummed after two or three days of painting and hundreds of smackers spent on a room you can no longer bear to enter. I have, for my spiritual well-being, repainted entire rooms on several occasions.

To further confuse you, paint store employees invariably, and with authority, claim that paint reads *lighter* on the wall than in the can.

"What's going on??"

Even *whites* are deceptive!

Paint itself is just WEIRD, actually one of life's seven great mysteries.

LESSON : TEST paint colors beforehand. Interior and exterior. It's worth the extra time and money.

LESSON : Or preserve your mental health and lengthen your lifespan, and stay with one pleasing off-white choice for ALL the rooms of your rental.

Also note that painters charge a fortune now. Once classified as "manual labor," they've become artisans—keenly aware that it's no longer easier, smarter, or cheaper for home-owners to do it themselves.

But make sure you hire good painters.

Okay, so now it's years later and you're ready to freshen your walls again. In your overalls and reading glasses, you're in your utility closet full of dusty-rusty, half filled paint cans, scrutinizing the situation.... Shucks, what a scene. Who knows what's in those cans?

Unless you still have the same helper from your original painting foray, any new worker on hand will simply lift each can, feel its weight, shake it for no reason, then cast aside any cans half empty or less, and chirp, "Just buy more!"

Why doesn't he value that leftover paint the way you do?

Well, we probably all agree that old paint down to the dregs is pretty useless, definitely that last inch or two at the bottom (that we hang onto anyway, just in case <u>your lame</u>

<u>reason here</u>   ). Too, your worker knows the time suck of trying to identify what's what in your closet and/or the likely futility of trying to "touch up" instead of repainting whole rooms. And all workers, of course, are freer with your money than theirs.

"But…but…but paint costs $60 to $110 a can nowadays," you collapse into your turquoise plastic Adirondack chair from Home Depot. The one tenants haven't broken yet.

"Everything's more expensive now," retorts the millennial worker, as if you're the inexperienced young person. "That's just the way it is."

But wait a sec…. This paint job under debate is *your* show, on *your* dime, in *your* house! You might save hundreds by using those paint remnants. Truth is, paint, even when it looks funky with the lid off, actually lasts quite a while. And if the look of it having settled over time doesn't repulse you completely, some paint reincarnates with a good stir. So before deferring to helpers paid by the hour, who'll predictably advise you to spend more, sort through your stash *alone* to evaluate what's usable. If stirring it well restores proper texture, you can, at the very least, use that paint as primer, or trim, or inside a closet, or for patching a ding somewhere, or even for art projects or yard sale signs.

You'll undoubtedly be buying new paint, too, unless you've religiously labeled your leftovers and truly know what's what on those shelves. And who doesn't love dipping their brush into a creamy tub of gasp-worthy gorgeousness? But paint's expensive, so don't waste it.

LESSON : Paint has become a precious commodity. So don't automatically be put off by the shabby look of a paint can or of the paint within—it might be usable.

However, in light of all the brouhaha and opposing opinions about leftover paint, paint colors, and the cost of paint, professional landlords, almost without exception, go off-white. It's the landlord color because this crowd knows there will be endless painting and repainting, and if they vary colors from room to room, and/or unit to unit, then try to store all those cans somewhere and keep track of everything, they'll go mental.

I'm just clueing you in. In my case, as you may have guessed, each room had to have its own unique feel. So I selected a breathy array of peaceful pastels. And you can imagine all the partially filled cans to be stored, when I could've opted for one milky five-gallon bucket of smart stuff.

For your sanity and your wallet, go off-white. There are a couple of preferred tints the pros lean into, and paint stores will readily share those favorites with you.

Another of life's seven great mysteries (who knew two of them pertained to home repair?) is why those color code stick-ons that paint stores slap onto the lid of your fresh gallon, either get covered by paint drips, wear off, get dusty in your shed, fade completely in a matter of months, or get discarded with the paint can after you finish the job. Additionally, the store usually dabs a blotch of the color on the lid, for you to identify at a glance. Thank you so much. For about a week. Later on (years), when you're ready to repaint, the can you're searching for is "somewhere" in your cryptic collection. Color dabs on lids are moldy grey now. And although the partially readable outer labels on the cans may still offer some vague data, you have zero recall what's inside. "Was it satin or flat? Interior or exterior? Behr Premium from Home Depot, or did I get it at Sherwin-

Williams?" Early-onset dementia creeps in as you rifle through your cruddy shelves and scold yourself for not fastidiously labeling each can then filing duplicates of the stats with your birth certificates and baby pictures. ("That's Jason learning to walk, and that's cute little Caitlyn, and that's Herb Medley, the color code for the master bedroom.")

LESSON : Whenever you complete a painting project, use a hammer or mallet to tightly re-seal your cans, and don't wait long to do it. Then, with indelible ink, mark all leftover paint cans as boldly and concisely as humanly possible. I write on blue painters' tape with a Sharpie: "INT. flat/ pink/ bdrm #2." Do it yourself rather than leaving it to a helper, who, bet on it, has unreadable handwriting. You'll be glad later. (Homer did it in my early landlord days. But when it mattered, years later, I couldn't decipher his microscopic chicken-scratch.)

And don't forget, when the earthquake, flood, or fire comes, grab that sacred paint documentation before even your pets! Better yet, bury it under the mango tree.

Worth Doing Well

Although construction is the absolute last field I ever expected to become proficient in, I learned the language. No building project intimidates me anymore. I mean, I wouldn't take on a suspension bridge, power generating dam, or even a skyscraper over forty floors, but in terms of home improvement and home maintenance, brang it. I know how to estimate and map out a project, how to interview and hire people, I know the tools and terminologies, how to manage workers, how to pay for it all, how to avoid BS, how to complete the job, and how to ultimately make it pay off. I also know how to emotionally and psychologically survive the ordeal.

So then…lo…one afternoon, I peered down the long hallway in the front unit, and *saw the light*! Literally SAW the light. After almost five months of that dark wood and unkempt dreariness, the hallway was painted white! And out from the bedroom doorways fluttered hints of pastel, like flowery aromas.

This project had been so all-encompassing from day one that I'd never dared envision it finished (like picturing your newborn a CEO). So it really threw me when I suddenly realized…there wasn't that much left to do. Normally, just looking at my clipboard would direct the business of the day, but now, heck, we were down to minor cosmetics like hanging curtain rods and adding outdoor plants. That glowing lightness in the hallway verified that the transformation was happening, this wreck of a property was becoming something quite different. It was becoming a nice house! Star of the neighborhood, in fact, with flowers a-blossom in every direction.

Could it really BE we were almost done? Was I forgetting a bunch of things? Was it possible I'd only need my workers a few more days? Geez, better sit down and ponder my new identity if I wouldn't be a butch GC anymore. No work force? No macho gatherings at the job-site every day?

Nope, I'd seen the light. My financial and employee dramas would be in the can. And my daily life would be at my own residence now. How totally bizarre.

But did I even remember how to be a girl? What do they wear? And wait, don't I get a diploma or something? A medallion for strength and courage, a badge? Maybe a little ceremony at the White House?

I gazed over every inch of the house to make doubly, triply sure I wasn't neglecting anything before I cut the boys loose. But the fact was we were DONE.

There would still be plenty to grapple with—my life would be nothing like before. Just being a homeowner was still new to me, not to mention two homes and a dog! I'd continue having tons of responsibility, Himalayas of debt, and real estate in the fantasy tropics, an ocean away from loved ones. Plus I'd soon be wingin' it as a landlady, starting any day now. But I'd been on island seven months, my massage business was percolating again, and Homer would be around to lend a hand.

So, from a local bakery, I ordered a huge sheet cake in the shape of a house. And on it, was written:

PAU HANA!
MAHALO!

In Hawaiian, that means, "Work Finished! Thank You!" And I brought it to the property for our celebration. Homer, Johnny, Kelvin and George, Rudy (the gardener who said I should've winked), and Rosie all partook of it.

And the next day, I ordered another giant house-shaped cake. On this one was written, "Mahalo to Everyone at Home Depot." And I took it to the store for those awesome employees to tear through in minutes flat. (They could've devoured three of them.)

Part III

The Landlord Hat

☰ *12* ☰

Gotta Be Local

Most people seek jobs based on their interests and skills, joy quotient, pay, and maybe promotional possibilities. They weigh proximity to where they live, hours they'll put in, and job title. They start fresh employment after careful deliberation about how they'll resonate with the new tasks, new mission, and new co-workers. With landlording though, one frequently falls into it without foreknowledge of the work detail. "You collect rent checks and deposit them into your account, right?"

Though it's rarely nine-to-five (unless remodeling, then it's five-to-nine), and though there may be interims when we're completely off the hook, even for several months, landlording is by no means a side hustle. In normal jobs, when you're done, you go home, but landlords are never totally in the clear. You can get calls at 6 a.m. or 10 p.m. if a refrigerator breaks, or "We're divorcing," or the roof springs a leak. And despite whose fault it is when things go askew, the remedy's not partly on you and partly on the tenants, but fully on you. You alone are responsible for everything that happens on that property. Plus you have to start problem solving on a dime…while the tenants await your solution, with their frozen food thawing out and their minds racing as to how they'll counter, should you choose to blame *them*.

Eager to fill my units, I advertised and started interviewing, looking for "the right people." First-time landlords envision renters who are upwardly mobile, clean, and personable, and who stay for years, even improving the place. I also had additional criteria in mind. I didn't want very young children because I couldn't bear seeing our hard work trashed. Nor did I want party animals, nor hopefully more than four residents in the three-bedroom front unit. Also, I had a charitable credo pertaining to my new community: "I don't want to be part of the problem." My uneducated view of "the problem" was new people moving to Hawai'i and taking housing away from locals, as well as newcomers changing the island demographics and culture—squeezing out locals, financially and culturally. Qualifying as part of the problem myself, I wanted to also be part of the solution. So I'd rent to locals at a fair price. I'm not trying to sound like the good guy, this just seemed like the right thing.

LESSON : Different sized units attract different family configurations. A three-bedroom will usually bring families with children, where a one-bedroom draws singles or couples.

But note that couples procreate. So don't be surprised if you end up with a pregnancy, then an infant. And btw, it's rarely confided in the interview when a woman is two or three months' pregnant. So you may sign a year lease, and six months later, they've got twins.

I drew up an application page that requested: full names of all occupants, dates of birth, social security numbers of adults, previous address (usually where they currently resided), present jobs, pets, vehicles, references—personal and work—and the question, "May we check your credit score?"

Regarding credit scores, there's a fee to check it. And since I was never comfortable paying it myself nor charging applicants, I didn't follow through on that. I figured if they didn't mind me checking their credit, it was probably decent.

For my front unit, I settled on two "local kine" women, newly arrived from O'ahu. Both about thirty, one was the manager at Taco Bell, the other the manager at Radio Shack. They said they were step-sisters and one had a six-year-old child. I'm thinkin', "Okay, local people, both have good jobs, they're family so they know each other well, they're not drinkers, and they only have one child who isn't a toddler." Plus they only had one vehicle.

They were staying in a hotel because they'd had trouble finding a place. Understandable, as Kaua'i housing is an expensive and tricky proposition.

So I signed on the little family for a year. They were delighted, handed over the moolah, got the key and moved in next morning.

I admit to palpable separation anxiety when, overnight, I lost all access to my cherished property, *my baby,* but at least Phase One was complete. Phase Two would have a whole different vibe—less chaotic, much cleaner, and no more debating everything. Not to mention money would be flowing in the proper direction and I wouldn't have to report to work at 7 a.m. every day.

That first evening, partly out of habit of constantly going over there and partly to be a responsible landlady, I did a drive-by to check that the ladies had moved in. Since it was after twilight, the lights were ablaze inside and, of course, no curtains were up yet. But as I slowly passed the house, what to my wondering eyes should appear in the front bedroom window? A gaggle of children joyfully jumping on a bed. Not two kids, not three, but LOTS! Bouncing up and down, squealing with glee.

But…since it was nighttime, and since I was mildly in shock…I let it be…for the moment.

Day one of being a landlady.

Next morning…oh brother, I went to Taco Bell and pulled into the take-out window. "Is Veronica here?" I asked the employee.

"No, she's off today."

"Oh, she's off?"

"Yeah. She went to the beach with her five kids."

"Five?"

"Yeah, she has five kids."

"Okay…well…thanks very much."

Day two of being a landlady.

All I knew was: a) I didn't want five children living in that house. I just spent months and eighty grand creating a palace and wouldn't have cookie-crunchers destroying it; and b) these women flat out lied, saying they had one child when they had five. I phoned Veronica (actually a sweet woman) and said we had to meet that same afternoon.

Sitting down sheepishly, she confessed that they'd lied because they'd been unable to find *anything* to rent. No landlords would take them with their five kids. And they had become desperate since they were spending a fortune staying in the hotel.

Who couldn't sympathize? "But I'm not at all comfortable with you lying to me," I said, "Didn't you know I would find out? I mean, how did you think this was going to play out?"

"Well, we figured we'd let you know…. But we just had to get a place so we could get on with our jobs and our lives—we were really stuck."

"Well, I'm not a hard-hearted person…but I don't want five little children in that house that I just restored. Plus we've got a double whammy because you also lied. So, let me think about it all…."

During the exchange, it was also revealed that the step-sister wasn't a step-sister after all, but the lesbian lover. Lie number two.

"We'll meet again tomorrow," I said, "to discuss what we're going to do."

At that point, they mentioned one option might be to send a couple of the kids back to their grandma on O'ahu.

"Well, you need to give it serious thought. Because we can't go forward with five kids in the house. I'll let you out of the lease if you want."

That night, I too thought hard about it. But despite compassion, I had to conclude that their jam wasn't remotely my issue, but entirely theirs.

"Okay, " I said the following day, "Here's the deal: you can stay, with three children. But you can't stay with five. I'm sorry. I'm bending over backwards to accommodate you and the fact that you lied. But three kids are all I'll accept." (I didn't know what else to do.) "Of course I'm sorry it's coming to this, but as the landlord, my job is to protect and maintain my property and honor our lease. That means following the terms we agreed to."

With hangdog demeanors, the ladies accepted my decree and elected to send two kids back to Granny. It had to be. Knowing it would be tough for them, I said that I would permit them, at any point, to end their lease early (with thirty days' notice to me) should they decide to move back to O'ahu or if they found a more lenient landlord on Kaua'i.

Day three of being a landlady—splitting up a young family!

I'd also just enlisted my first tenant for the back unit. Randall, a recently divorced man of thirty-five, had two children he was passing to and fro with his ex. He was local, per my bias, not too rough around the edges and, to my surprise, a pastor. (Before I met numerous clergy members through my massage business, I was still swayed by implications of "the cloth." I now know that, like every other walk of life, that gang is a mixed bag. The excellent perks that ministries offer—like free housing and monster tax breaks— can attract anglers. If I sound cynical, it's because I am.)

Randall moved in the back, where his kids would join him half the week.

And all the while, I was trying from six miles away to "feel" how the property-sharing of the two units was working out—parking arrangements, noise factors, separation of front and back yards. Was the plumbing okay, the electricity? Was everything going as planned?

The two ladies and three remaining kids ended up returning to Oʻahu about three months later. But they left the place clean and got back their full deposit.

But my holy man also defaulted. Though he postured otherwise, his deposit and first month's rent turned out to be his full earthly holdings. So the second month, to my chagrin, he cruised on the fumes of his security deposit. Apparently, he'd strategized from the start that he could linger another month without paying, while giving the landlady a song and dance about looking for another place.

Later on, I'd come across Randall from time to time, working as a valet or sneaking into a pool at some condo complex where I was giving a massage—usually doing odd things that didn't altogether dovetail with his alleged calling.

LESSON : Leases boldly dictate, "Security deposit may not be used as last month's rent." Because if that deposit gets burned as rent, the landlord has zip to cover damages, unpaid rent, and/or cleaning after tenants vacate. Plus you're uneasy that entire unpaid month because who knows if they will, in fact, move out? Money has power over people. And without financial collateral, people may not play ball. With no funds coming back to them, tenants don't *need to* clean up before departing, or even remove their piles of trash.

The "security deposit" is so named because it's a landlord's only *security*, our stash to fix things tenants break, to clean up, and to cover any unpaid rent. *LESSON :* A full one-month security deposit should be collected with every new lease, and all the guidelines pertaining to it honored to a tee.

   LESSON : Also, make sure you have that entire sum on hand at refund time. And, aside from legitimate losses and damages, make a firm habit of returning the money in full and on time.

   My first two tenant trials equated to having to start over now in both units.

13

More Open-minded

I was zero for two—two sets of local tenants, two lies, two defaults. Perhaps "locals only" wasn't the most genius landlord formula. Oh alright, maybe I'm the only landlord in history who ever went that route. Others opted for the lightest, smallest possible footprint in their units—a female preferable to a male (cleaner), an older person preferable to a young rocker (quieter). And of course, all landlords adhered religiously to "no smokers" and "no pets." Avoiding drinkers was harder to drill down. And sussing who was on pills or freaky meds was virtually impossible.

"Okay, new credo," I recalibrated my m.o. "Trying to house locals" would have to give way to "not wanting to repeat gnarly experiences." And I decided, "Going forward, I'm just gonna look for the Best Tenant, that's it. No more preferences, just best candidate! I don't care if they're purple or from Jupiter."

LESSON : Discriminate! Screen the heck out of your prospects. Get them talking, they'll reveal things, "We have three cars and an RV." Throwaway remarks like that will only emerge at the end of a lengthy convo. (And all these vehicles might be fine with you, but you need to be apprised.)

Again, I advertised and met with applicants.

For the front, this time I selected Jerri, a seventy-four-year-old haole Mainlander who'd been on the island a couple of years. She was an educated lady who'd come to Hawai'i to live out her retirement plan. Currently residing in a one-bedroom apartment in a senior community, she wanted more space so her two grown kids in California could pay extended visits.

"Ideal. Just one person. And a single older woman." I was relieved.

Jerri was slim—which I took to mean active, though hardly a gym rat—and though she casually mentioned having emphysema, she seemed spunky. So we signed the lease and she paid her deposit and first month's rent.

"Let me know if you need any help moving," I said. "My handyman, Homer, is very reasonable and nice."

"I think I'm okay. I'll make a lot of trips," she said. With her apartment only a mile away, this seemed manageable.

Every day or two, I'd drive by to see how the move was progressing, but nothing appeared to be happening—no curtains, no car in driveway, no signs of activity. I figured, as a retiree, Jerri probably was in no rush.

But when a full week passed, I gave her a call, "Hi Jerri, I'm just checking in because it looks like you haven't moved in yet. Everything okay? Need any help?"

"Oh yeah, yeah, everything's fine. I'm just gettin' all my stuff together, gettin' ready."

"Well, I don't want to be bothering you, and of course you can take your time, but feel free to call me if you need help."

"Okay."

I then concentrated on the back unit, and reeled in a young, unmarried, local couple. Both had jobs and came across as content and compliant.

But I kept an eye on the front. And when two more weeks passed with no movement, I phoned Jerri again. And she amiably repeated that she'd be moving in soon.

Well…as long as she was paying the rent and not causing problems, she could do as she pleased….

But by and by, the next month arrived and I didn't receive the rent or hear anything from my ghostly tenant.

I wasn't sure what to do now. Our lease stated, "Tenant must pay by noon on the 3rd of the month or be charged a late fee." So, needing Jerri to pay so I didn't have to stress, I phoned her on the 3rd, thinking I'd remind her to avoid the late fee. But she didn't answer. So I left a message to that effect and said I'd stop by her apartment that afternoon to pick up the check.

I was familiar with her apartment complex and had the unit number, so I swung by later that day and gave a knock on the door.

Opening it, Jerri seemed a bit frailer than before. Leaning against the doorjamb, she explained that she wasn't feeling well. "Would it be alright if I just send you the check?" she asked.

Was she literally too ill to write out a check, or stalling for more time? Neither eased my concerns. "It would be best to give me a check while I'm here. Then it's done, and you avoid the late fee."

She still put me off, "I really don't feel well…."

Without her payment, however, I wouldn't feel well either. And though persisting was awkward, Jerri wasn't divulging *when* she intended to pay. Also, if she didn't want to pay me when I was standing in her doorway (three days after the rent was due), it seemed doubtful things would be reversing in my favor.

This occasion—not dissimilar to telling Veronica she had to send two of her kids back to O'ahu—was a come-to-Jesus, landlord smack. It's awful to be rigid with people facing weighty personal issues. What should I do or say?

But the truth was, I simply had to do *my job*. A huge piece of landlording is protecting your property, yourself, and your investment. You're in the wrong game if you cave to tenant mishaps, tough or gut-wrenching as they may be.

LESSON : Tenant problems cannot become your problems, or your goose is cooked. Certain concessions may be made now and then, if tenants acknowledge their own responsibilities regarding the lease. But in Jerri's case, as in Veronica's, they'd overextended by renting my house. Both had, intentionally or un-, pulled an innocent bystander (the landlord) into their major life issues. And despite their hurdles and my own emotions, getting ensnared in their dramas would be disastrous for me.

"I'm so sorry you're not well," I had to say to Jerri, "but the rent is still due. And since I'm here, it's probably easier to write a check right now. Then hopefully, you'll get some rest after I leave."

With surrender, she wrote the check.

I felt bad taking it, but rent collection is foundational to landlording. I just hoped she'd rally and make the move soon.

But to make sure no financial upsets topped off whatever else was going on, I took the check to her bank and cashed it.

I remained concerned though, and a couple of days later phoned again to see how she was doing.

No answer, so I again left a message.

Jerri didn't call back. So I decided to go by again to see if she needed anything. I could easily get her some food or whatever else she might want.

At her place, I knocked lightly on the door.

No answer.

Knocked again.

Then I knocked a third time, louder, and called out, "Are you home, Jerri?" If she was in, she would've heard me.

But I then noticed a few rolled-up newspapers by the door.

So I went down to the manager's office, "You know, there's a resident here who I'm a bit concerned about. She didn't respond to my phone message and she's not answering her door. She's a bit older and wasn't feeling well. Can you enter her apartment or somehow help me find out if she's okay?"

"No, I can't. It's her business. And we're not going in there."

"But I'm actually *really* concerned about her. And I know she doesn't have anyone keeping track of her. She doesn't have any relatives here, her people are on the Mainland."

"No, we're not going to do that."

With mild disbelief, I shrugged and left his office.

Going back upstairs, I stood outside Jerri's door, sensing that now this really had become my problem because my tenant was MIA. That's when I noticed flies buzzing around.

Glancing at adjacent units, I spotted an open door, so I knocked on the screen.

A kindly older gent let me in. "Do you know Jerri?" I asked.

"Yeah, I do."

"Have you seen her lately?"

He thought a second, "No, not in a couple of days."

"Well, I'm worried about her. She hasn't returned my call, and there are newspapers by her door…. And there are some flies buzzing around…. She's not super healthy, and I'm…concerned."

We strolled together back to Jerri's door. "I agree," he said, "this doesn't look good."

"I went down to the manager's office," I said, "but he won't help and says he can't let me in."

"Well, I actually have a key to her place," said the guy. "She and I gave each other keys in case either of us ever got locked out."

At that point, a female neighbor walked by, someone who also knew Jerri. Now there were three of us with the same eerie feeling. We went back into the man's apartment. "Let's just sit down at the table for a moment," I suggested, "and decide the best thing to do."

So we sat. It was clear that if we didn't take action, no one else was going to. "I just want us to all be in agreement," I said slowly, "about what we're about to do. I think we need to agree that we *should* go into the apartment and *why* we're going in."

They nodded, "Yeah, we should all agree that we just needed to check her status."

"But," I said, "if she's…not alive, then what do we do?"

"I guess we call the police," said the guy.

"Yeah," I agreed, "and tell them we mutually decided to go in there. Because, otherwise, it might seem strange that we were in her apartment." (Somebody watches too much *Dateline*.)

We returned to Jerri's door and knocked again. When no one answered, the guy stuck his extra key in the lock and cracked open the door. He called inside for Jerri, but there was no response. So he opened the door fully and stepped in. He then turned around to us, "It doesn't smell good in here."

And we knew.

"I'm gonna hang back," I said, staying outside while the guy entered slowly and started looking around.

He continued into the darkened living room, as the neighbor woman tentatively followed. Seeing no one, they proceeded down the hallway toward the bedroom and bathroom. The man looked into the bedroom, "No one in there." Then he stepped into the bathroom.

After a brief pause, he called out, "She's in here. She's dead."

I didn't press for details, but recall him saying that it seemed she'd been there a while, more than a day.

We summoned the police, who swiftly arrived.

It was good we'd synced our story because the cops could see we were just three citizens checking on a neighbor. (Though on *Dateline* we would've been persons of interest.)

Obviously Jerri had been terribly unwell, probably doubted she'd live out the month. I was to learn she'd been a heavy smoker, too, and had sort of fudged that interview question.

But I now had to phone her daughter, and everything proceeded from there, the daughter and son arriving days later. And since Jerri had paid the rent, they could use my rental as base camp. I brought over some chairs and household staples for them, and the unit served as their retreat from the serious business they had at their mother's apartment.

Of course, the son and daughter wanted Jerri's security deposit from me, as well as reimbursed rent for the remainder of the month after they left. (It's amazing how simplistic the landlord reality appears to outsiders.) And, obviously, I'd be fair. But I could only reimburse them for any days I managed to install new tenants, hopefully to finish out the month. I explained that I'd start interviewing as soon as the son and daughter vacated and the place was empty. Plus, I said they'd pretty surely get the full deposit back.

Fortunately, Jerri's kids were courteous, though couldn't quite grasp that new tenants aren't pulled out of a hat like a magic trick. And with cash probably coming back to them, they left the place clean. Luckily, I did get new renters quickly, so *per diem* funds for the remainder of that month accompanied their full deposit check.

Still, cold as it sounds, I was grateful I'd gotten Jerri's check that day—so her kids could use the place, and so I didn't have to cover more than half a month's rent myself or seem cruel if I'd had to keep the deposit.

⚏ ⚏ ⚏ ⚏

My rental credo now morphed from "best candidates, any flavor" to "absolutely anyone who is *straight up*. I don't care if they're a land developer, a hit-man from Brooklyn, or they're building weapons for outer space—if they can pay the rent, rationally communicate with me, don't drink, can outlive their lease, and aren't moving extended family in, they get the place." An elaborate credo.

So I got some traveling nurses for the front. The pros about traveling nurses are: They're clean and hardworking, so won't be hosting beer pongs; since they don't know anybody locally, they won't move boyfriends in; their agency reliably pays the rent and on time; and since the nurses aren't paying anything themselves, they question nothing and view you as a nice auntie. You sign them on for three months, they stay for three months, and that's it. And sometimes they extend their stay.

The cons might be: You have strangers living together (though traveling nurses are accustomed to amalgamation); they favor three-month leases; knowing nothing about the community, they don't particularly care about it; they're generally quite young; and, in Hawai'i, we don't wear shoes indoors, but Mainlanders don't readily conform to the custom. Finally, the agency reports to the IRS, so you get a 1099 at year's end.

I had no problem with the nurses, and did two rounds of them. But three months passes quickly, and such rapid turnover, ultimately, wouldn't work for me.

I advertised again and now scored the perfect tenant— one of maybe two to ever cross that front threshold. Scott was the bomb, from the day we met right up to our tearful farewell. Clean-cut and about thirty, he was new to the island, had a high-paying job, and sought a residence near his workplace. There was only one minor hitch…but, thanks to my updated preferences, no longer a hindrance: Scott was a *bomb-maker.* He worked for Raytheon, the stealthy-wealthy folk who build weapons for outer space.

On principle, a *bomb designer* would not be my choice tenant. In *this* reality, however, such smallness as intergalactic warfare could be dismissed. (Plus, I could put him on speed dial for when the Martians invaded.)

Ironically though, and war mongering aside, Scott was the most easygoing tenant I ever had and a much needed breath of fresh air. He was healthy, athletic, hardworking, overjoyed at being on Kaua'i, and wanted nothing more than carefree weekends to explore the island.

Things went well for a spell—Scott in front, the couple in back. I got heavily into walking my fantastic dog; paying down mortgages, equity loans, and Home Depot debt; poring over my spread sheets; teaching yoga and doing record-breaking numbers of massages islandwide.

But just a few months after Scott moved in, his aerospace patron offered him a job in Texas that he couldn't refuse. Though he passionately wanted to stay, and swore he'd be back someday, the new contract was too lucrative. "If you let me out of the lease," he offered, "I'll pay for all of next month, plus you can keep the deposit. And if you find somebody else in the meantime, you don't have to reimburse me, just keep that extra money."

That, by the way, is how to handle breaking a lease.

"Okay," said I, "fair deal. And I truly wish you the best. You've been a great tenant and I'm sad you're leaving. I hope you do come back. Call me when you do. Maybe you'll rent from me again."

Not only did Scott do as he'd promised, and left the place immaculate, but he gave me his brand new queen bed, that I sleep on to this day.

LESSON : As a landlord, it's not your job to take the moral high ground. Let people do what they do. Your job is to maintain the property, collect the rent, and keep *decent people* in your place.

The young couple in back was fine...until their relationship fizzled. Then, according to neighbors, there was shouting. And when their lease ended, they separated and moved out, sending me back to the drawing boards there, as well.

More than a year had now passed since I bought the house. And again, I needed new tenants, front and back.

The good news was that property values were climbing, suggesting my investments were sound. Each of my houses had appreciated over $100,000. And despite the half mil I owed the world, my net worth was growing.

☷ ☷ ☷ ☷

Many arriving on tropical islands are giddy, if not delirious, having left all their problems back on the Mainland. It's just a fact that if you have complaints in Paradise, there's something wrong with you. And psycho-spiritually, lots of newcomers also feel they've "been called to the island," are "manifesting their destiny," and "finally living the life they deserve." There's almost a tune to these recurring chants. Some claim they're here to heal the unevolved masses, lead everyone to the light, coach the uninspired in ecstatic dance or bowl-chiming, or use unpronounceable therapies to cure vexed carnivores. At the very least, they'll supply our pathetic rock with more vegan recipes, and/or massage, and/or marketing for your entrepreneurial vision (they'll turn your website pinkish purple in exchange for living on your property). (Think Andrew.) Many of these self-described "sweet couples" or "loving families"— with no means, but shamanic prowess in spades and several fur babies—seek work/trade arrangements, where they'll inhale your largesse while tending your fruit trees. (Fruit trees, btw, don't need tending.) Their offerings actually make you pine for good old astrologers and Tarot readers.

Fresh off the boat, Carolyn was as high on Hawai'i as anyone. A single black lady from SoCal, and another ain't-life-grand dreamer, she had more credibility than many because she was financially flush and pushing fifty. So I took her for the back unit.

Because she was mature, and knew no one on island, I tried to make her feel at home by letting her recount how she'd sold her Mainland house and was now going to do nothing but sniff plumeria blossoms. "It's ME time!" she freed Orange County from her soul. "I'm gonna have Carolyn time! I'm gonna spend entire days on the beach just having Carolyn time!"

My new lodgers in front were a man, his second wife, and their five-year-old boy. Though they placed hundreds of tiny seashells around the garden (that took me years to remove), they proved excellent tenants…until they bought their own house and bailed on the lease. "Oh, they were nice and they found a house," I fell for the recurring theme of people swapping out their Mainland homes for the tropical fantasy, and just needing a short-term perch from which to scout for that beachfront hovel that no one else seems to want.

But their vacating made Carolyn even more expansive, "I need more space!" she sang. "I think I'll move into that front unit now." She could afford more elbow room, or maybe thought her kids would visit, so her mind was made up. And it was fine with me to have only one resident in front.

Carolyn, however, turned out to be…. Well, in just a matter of weeks, she started flailing when left to her own devices. Banking on island magic to keep her happy, and having expected more of a social scene on Kaua'i, she grew lonely, then more and more restless. So she'd call me and ask if I knew about this or that, and even hired me twice to come give her massages. I listened to the unraveling of her illusions, and offered comfort. In retrospect, though, I'd wager Carolyn was on some sort of pills. She ended up despondent and out of sorts, not knowing what to do or even where to go. And since she didn't have or need a job, after a mere few months, she concluded Paradise was overrated, she missed her kids, and she was going home. Though she bailed on the lease without much notice, she understood she'd sacrifice her deposit.

14

The Application Process

In the unfolding of my landlord career, half the time I felt like a social worker, the other half like I was enrolled in some dark mystic field of study (and failing).

But what became clearer by the year was that—aside from following your state's landlord/tenant guidelines and maintaining clean, well-functioning living quarters—a landlord's most important responsibility is securing the best possible renters. Thus, screening applicants is key. Why? Because they can fool you. Also, all people have two sides, and the good dogs on interview day can become very bad bow-wows once snugly under your roof.

That being said, what follows will seem slanted against tenants—as if no one can be trusted and everyone's a loser. But "forewarned is forearmed" is the total premise of this book, and these scenarios just illustrate how far south things can veer.

The Power

During the application process is when certain factors are to your advantage. While selecting your next tenants, and at that moment *only,* you're in the power seat. Here are some guidelines for that process:

1. Applicants are, customarily, on good behavior. Notice how nicely they're dressed. They need a place to live and you're offering one. Sometimes they really, really want it, other times they don't have many options and this might work—like you take pets and most other landlords don't. Bottom line, unless they're true low-lifes or have something to hide, therefore can't survive the interview, they're being polite and will indulge your questions.

2. Because home hunters may be in a tight spot, you could be pivotal to their destiny. Maybe your property's location or price is right for them, maybe they like the short lease and/or that you accept dogs, maybe they need something quickly, maybe they're desperados (bad credit, felonies, jail terms, HUD, lousy work history, you name it) and other landlords won't take them. But the minute you hand over the key, the power becomes theirs. So accomplish everything you can whilst in control. In other words, *drag out the interview.* With their filled-out application in hand, first disarm them by asking benign, friendly questions. They have no inkling they'll be sitting with you more than a couple of minutes.

LESSON : Never rent to anyone based solely on a ten-minute walk-through and filled-out application. An additional fifteen minutes on the front end can save you fifteen weeks of time, energy, and headaches later. Let your applicants know, "I never rent a place without an interview. I have a series of questions that are important to me and I'm sure you have some, too." Should they balk at being questioned, just say, "That's okay. I totally understand. And you're in no way obliged to answer questions. I've got your application. Thank you so much for stopping by."

3. Never feel pressured to make a decision. If someone's in a giant rush and pushes for your decision, keep control. Say anything that grants you time to make your decision with clarity, like "I've got a couple more interviews scheduled for today and tomorrow, and I told them I won't rent the place until they've seen it."

An aside: Once, when I was seeking a roommate to live in my own home with me, a young woman on the Mainland responded to my Craigslist ad. After a few minutes on the phone though, I sensed she wasn't someone I'd be comfortable sharing space with. Not wanting to waste time, I indicated why the place might not work for her. But she liked the price and location (and needed a landing place), so she persisted. And when I repeated that I wasn't sure it would work, she got snooty, "You know, I really don't want to have a power struggle with you."

So here's someone who wants to live *with me*, in *my* house, using all *my* furniture, *my* linens, *my* kitchen equipment, and within three minutes already has attitude. "It's not a power struggle," I replied, "I have all the power."

BUT *only* when they're an applicant is that the case.

Getting back to the process…. So, you advertise on Craigslist or wherever, offering a rent amount you deem appropriate. But if over the course of the next week, you get only a few calls, this may suggest your price is too high (unless it's a sleepy market). And definitely, if everyone who phones has two dogs or seven occupants (i.e. few landlords want them), you'll need to lower the rent. Once I understood how the number of responses correlates to the rent amount, I'd usually kick off with an optimistic price to test the waters.

But realize, too, that after owning a property for a number of years, it's possible to lose track of the going rate. Rents may have gone up a few hundred per month without your knowing, or gone shockingly down, as in a recession. Rates roll in both directions and may fluctuate broadly over a span of years.

So first you screen 'em on the phone. My spiel went like this: "Thank you for calling. May I ask you a few questions about your household?"

"Sure."

I'd then run through my questions and carefully register their replies.

Since a ton of info is being requested, in this day and age more than ever, it's legit for people to feel hesitant about divulging sensitive factoids over the phone. So you must be jolly, polite, and discreet, otherwise they'll get bristly and turned off. "Why are you asking me so many questions? We haven't even seen the house!"

Still, it's universally understood that answering personal questions is the only way to secure a new rental. So if you're offering something nice, reasonably priced, and you're cordial and fair, put forth your questions and don't second-guess yourself. For every generic query of yours, some other landlord is asking tougher ones, has more severe restrictions, and charges for credit reports. Few landlords take pets, some won't take children, many insist on cleaning deposits, and many won't rent for less than a year. Also, some units are plain yucky, some have ludicrous prices, some have landlords living upstairs or barking dogs next door, and some are smack on the highway or out in the boonies.

But some callers will definitely opine, "You're asking too many personal questions." And if they got ruffled, I would just say, "I know I'm asking a lot of questions, but we want to cover any deal-breakers. And I want to answer your questions, too. We don't want to meet at the house then find out it won't work for some little reason we could've covered on the phone."

And those who can't take the heat might be alerting you that you wouldn't want them anyway. Getting prickly can mean they have something to hide. Cheekiness and/or aggression may also point to possible drinkers—tough to ask about directly. Bottom line, if you get pushback—like they're already challenging you after four minutes on the phone or won't share basic details about their household—you don't want them. Just say, "That's okay. I understand. Thank you so much for calling."

Click. Bullet dodged.

My basic phone questions were: "When do you need to move?" "Do you currently live on the island?" "If not, when are you arriving?" "Who will be living in your household, and what are their ages?" "Do you work?" "Does your spouse work?" "If so, where?" "How long have you been working there?" "Do you have any pets, and if so, what are they?" "Are there any smokers?" "How long a lease were you looking for?" "How many vehicles do you have? And what size are they?"

And indeed, if at first it feels outlandish to probe total strangers, just imagine housing anyone about whom you don't know the answers to those questions. You can't!

Each landlord's core questions will vary. For instance, if your rental has plenty of parking, vehicle details may not matter. But if you only have two spaces per unit, three adults will probably have three vehicles. And even if they say, "We only have two vehicles," one could be a giant truck, or they could acquire a third vehicle two weeks after move-in that there's no room for.

They also might say something like, "We do have three cars right now, but we're selling one. Is it okay if we keep it until we sell it?"

If you agree to that, let them know it will be spelled out in the lease or addendum, "Okay to have three cars for first month only. If vehicle is not sold, landlord may remove the third vehicle at tenants' expense." Because if you say, "Sure, no worries," it'll sit there for a year. Give tenants a centimeter, they'll take an acre. Then there's no guest parking available, the mailman can't pull up to the mailbox, the gardener can't mow under it, the car's dead, it's an eyesore, it's probably leaking oil, there's nowhere for you to park when you go over to prune the bushes, and it's blatantly unfair to other tenants on the property.

After your first round of questioning, if things are humming along, you might want to ask, "Is there anyone else who's planning to live with you or spend a lot of time at your house?" Never hurts to ask.

If they reply, "Oh, our daughter and her son are going to be living with us," that, in theory, may sound okay—three adults and one child—in a three-bedroom unit. But is this son six or twenty-six?

In this instance, there may be a further question, dare you ask, "Is there an ex-husband still in the picture?"

You're thinking, "Alcoholic wild card banging down the door while the baby's howling," while they're thinking, "This bitch is really meddling, she'll be an obnoxious landlord. But we're desperate so we gotta indulge her."

If it feels sticky, just repeat, "I know these are a lot of questions, but there may be something that really matters to you or to me that should be addressed before we schedule time to meet at the house." Remember, you still have the power.

Another important question is, "Why are you moving?"

A common Kaua'i response is, "Our landlord is selling the place where we currently live." But the fact that *so many* applicants give this same reason suggests it's not always true. What IS true, though—that they're inconsiderate, alcoholic, welfare-recipient musicians with dodgy relatives swarming day and night—probably won't win them an invite to your rental.

"Is it okay if I call your boss or current landlord for a reference?" you may also ask. Though, mind you, references aren't necessarily what they seem. Initially, I phoned whom-ever applicants wrote down. But after getting sparkling testimonies for borderline deadbeats, I realized that applicants only pony up references who'll speak well of them— sister, friend, paid employee. And those testimonials are worthless. *LESSON :* Testimonials from mothers and other relations are a wash.

Try to speak to previous landlords; they may be truthful. But even if a tenant's ex-landlady sings her praises, it's moot if the tenant's new live-in boyfriend is a drug dealer/addict.

Work references are a better bet. And if your call is answered, "Good morning, Toyota Service," that's a thumbs up.

But thumbs down if your applicant says, "I don't want you to call my workplace."

In the event that all their answers have satisfied you so far, (I always waited, usually in vain, for them to mention the c-word, for "clean"), then turn it over to them. "I'm sure you have questions for me, too, so go ahead."

Their questions may include, "When is it available?" "Does it have a yard?" "Are utilities included?" "Is it near a bus stop?" "Do you do month-to-month?" "Do you check credit scores?" "Is it a stand-alone unit or are there other rentals on the property?" "Can we do a drive-by?"

The longer you engage them, the more will be revealed. I had a woman tell me, at the *end* of our phone chat, "Yeah, every morning all my grandchildren get dropped off here and I have a little family daycare center." Five days a week, she babysat all her grandchildren in the rental unit while their parents went to work. But because her own kids didn't *live* with her, I never asked about *grandchildren* because they didn't enter my mind. And you might be fine with a daycare center for little cousins, but I wasn't.

You'll be surprised at what people can spill. "My sister's moving here to join us in June," or "Our seven-year-old is begging for a dog," or "We don't smoke cigarettes, just a little weed for pain relief." Casual for them, possible deal-breakers for you. "Since I'm a mechanic, I sometimes do jobs at home," or, "Oh, we do have several cats…."

"How many?"

"About five."

"*About* five?"

"Well, we think one might be pregnant."

And people can have unusual circumstances, in which case, finding a new residence is tough for them. Like the woman who casually asked, "Is it okay if I pasture a couple of horses in the yard?"

"Well, there's no fence…so that probably wouldn't work."

"Oh, that's okay, I have my own fencing."

So, let's peek in on a fairly typical Kaua'i interview:

"Hi, I'm calling about the house for rent?" The voice sounds like a mellow, local guy.

"Great. When are you guys looking to move?" (For a three-bedroom, you can assume there are several in the household.)

"Oh, we're ready right now. As soon as we find something."

"That's good, because the place will be empty in a couple of days."

"Yeah, when can we see it?"

"Well, do you mind if I ask you a few questions?"

"Yeah, sure, fire away."

"How many people are in your household?"

"Oh. Well…." When they pause to think about this, or to count, or to figure out how to break you the bad news…not good. It's either a fluctuating household, possibly with children passed in and out, or there are more people in their group than they think you'll want to hear about.

But you listen.

"Okay, so there's me…."

"Yeah…."

"My girlfriend…."

"Yeah…."

"And then we both have a coupla kids."

Take nothing at face value, especially words like "a coupla" or "a few" pertaining to people, pets, or vehicles. Or the word "sometimes," pertaining to their activities, or "might," pertaining to other relations jumping on the hayride.

LESSON : Get details about every aspect of their household, jobs, and lifestyle.

"So how many kids total?"

"Oh, total?" he chuckles. "Well…two of 'em are only there part-time. My kids."

"So you have two?"

"I have two, but only on Thursday, Friday and Saturday."

"And how many kids does she have?

"She has three."

"And they live there all the time?"

"Yeah, they live with her."

By now, I'm just being polite. (Even you, fair reader, already knows I don't want five kids.) But we mustn't appear "discriminating." Plus some of these family configurations are quite entertaining. So I might say, "So how old are her kids?"

"Her kids are, let's see, Jesse's three, Tammy's five, and then the big one, Jacob, is about nine."

"And how old are your kids?"

"My kids are older. They're fourteen and sixteen."

I visualize this, "So you've got five kids. And three are there all the time, and two are there Thursday, Friday, and Saturday?"

"That's right." He thinks this is going well.

And to be fair, these might be the nicest humans to ever walk this flat Earth, but that doesn't mean my small three-bedroom is equipped for them. Or that I want to rent to an unmarried couple.

But I might humor them a bit longer so as not to seem unfair, or to get a solid reason why I really can't take them. "So, how long have you guys been together?"

"Oh, we've been together like two years already."

"And do you both work?"

"Oh yes. Of course!"

"What do you do?"

"I work as a mechanic…and she got a lot of different jobs. She does housecleaning and she works with her mother over at the farm, and…she's always busy. She got lots going on."

"How many vehicles do you guys have?"

"We only have one vehicle. We try to keep it simple."

LOL, there's nothing remotely simple about a newly formed, unmarried couple with a blended household of seven. Everything he's shared suggests they're over-extended and running in place trying to manage all the kids. Yet the worst of this interview may be yet to come…. It's no mega surprise to learn the girlfriend's pregnant or that ornery exes are dropping off kids and bouncing alimony checks.

In this instance, the actual dialogue probably wouldn't've lasted this long. And any reader who hasn't lost count of the red flags might not be good landlord material. Because, once you know in your heart this won't work for you, even if they're the world's most unimposing people—and, believe me, sympathy creeps in—there's no point in stringing them along.

So now you have to steer the chat to some slam-dunk issue that may provide you an off-ramp.

"Are there any animals?"

"Well, I have dogs."

"How many?"

"Only two," he laughs.

You laugh too, so as not to cry. "What kind of dogs are they?"

"They're pit bull mix, but they're totally outdoor dogs and they have cages."

"Okay." Sigh. "Any other animals?"

"Just the dogs really. Except for a couple of cats, but they're…y'know…."

Believe it or not, on Kaua'i, nothing about this conversation, or this household, is unusual.

"Any other animals or people?" You conceal your early-onset fatigue.

"No."

"You sure? No mother-in-law, no parrots? No more kids? Sounds like you could use some livestock."

"Well, I mean, I have one grown-up kid, but he's… grown up! He lives on his own."

"Oh yeah, where does he live?"

"He lives with his mother over on the West Side."

"Does he have any kids?"

He laughs again. "Yeah, he does, but only part-time. And they're not my problem!"

"But they're your grandchildren…. How many does he have?"

Laughs again, "He's crazy, he has five!"

"And you don't see them?"

"Oh, I see them. I love them, they're my *family*! But I go out there, they never come here!"

Island life. Just keep asking, "Anybody else?" until they've owned up to every gecko, hamster on life support, part-time kid, and geriatric step-uncle. Sure, they might not find it prudent confessing their total population in a cursory phone interview, but a landlord needs the full whammy.

Then, census compiled, it's your decision what you and your property can tolerate.

LESSON : You may feel glum or compromised rejecting people, but if you go soft and "try to help them," or believe they're the only viable contenders out there, you're making a mistake.

Unless you're hungry for hard lessons or have excess spiritual reserves, don't make other people's problems your own. Select tenants whose lives seem under control and who exude a semblance of health, joy, family values, balance, solvency, and work ethics.

Also, you'll hear numerous potential renters proudly declare, "We always pay our rent!" or "We always pay our rent on time," as if that's the critical component. Odd as it sounds, payment of rent is no big deal for landlords, because anyone in default is evicted in a heartbeat. Even judges bang the gavel in two shakes over that one.

I'd always reply, "Thank you, but people who don't pay their rent aren't even on my radar."

And without exception, every caller will ask for the address of your rental—usually their first question—to do a drive-by. If you give it, though, they'll head over there the second you hang up. And if no cars are parked on the property (or sometimes even if they are), they'll hop out and possibly even look in the windows!

Because my rental neighborhood was notoriously lackluster, I had to seriously dissuade drive-bys. Plus I needed to be on hand for their first impressions, in order to explain how wonderful the neighbors were and how convenient the location. So on the phone, I'd say, "I don't give out the address before our appointment because I have tenants in there and I can't have anyone entering the premises to look around. Also, you can't even see half the house or the back yard from the street, so driving by doesn't give an accurate idea of the property."

Containing their annoyance, they'll vow not to get out of their car. "We just want to get a sense of the neighborhood."

That's when, if you feel okay about them otherwise, you agree to meet them over there as soon as humanly possible, even in half an hour. Unless you have tenants living there, to whom you must give twenty-four hours' notice. (Though I only showed my units empty.) If a same day meeting isn't possible, you can say, "We can meet there in the morning and I'll text you the address then." And since they're still being good dogs at this point, motivated applicants will begrudgingly go along with your program, as long as you make them comfortable.

So, you set up appointments to show the unit. People look around and, if interested, fill out an application.

Just know that this on-site interview, before you accept tenants, is probably the longest exchange you'll ever have with them, even if they live there for years. Because after they're in, you'll only see them in passing. So seize this opportunity to gather all final data *before* lease signing. The worst thing about landlording is what you discover *after* people move in—possibly just two days from now.

LESSON : An in-depth interview is critical. When applicants get comfy and chatty, much can be disclosed.

But few ~~applicants~~ humans are straight-shooters. Hence, should you meet one, s/he is golden. Like when they cut to the chase, "You know, we do smoke. We didn't want to tell you on the phone because we knew you wouldn't want to show the house to us." Or, "We have a boat that we take out of the water for the winter and we store it in our yard." Or, "Can we put up a fence so our dog can have run of the yard?"

All deal-breaker queries or responses should be addressed on the spot. I learned to simply say, "I'm really sorry, but I don't allow any kind of storage on the property. Do you have another place to keep your boat?"

"No."

"Okay, bye."

Why so hard line? Take that fence, for example. The minute tenants pay for something, it's *theirs*. A) They can take it away with them when they go, or, worse, not take it away when they go. B) They're the ones choosing the style of whatever it is they want, and they'll invariably choose the cheapest, ugliest product on the market. C) You've got your existing landscaping to consider and safeguard. D) You'll inevitably encounter neighbor issues pertaining to a fence.

LESSON : From my experience, you don't want people building stuff, storing stuff, or planting stuff. No fence, no shed, no vegetable garden, no fruit trees.

That's not to say there aren't plenty of tenants and landlords with symbiotic agreements where tenants add something to the property that's beneficial to the landlord. You could have a construction worker tenant willing to build you a deck. But such arrangements need to be VERY diligently negotiated and discussed in fine detail—including the timing, cost, payment or trade agreement, and duration of construction—and everything put in writing before proceeding. I personally would want to either help the tenant with the project or at least be present daily while it's in progress. In fact, I'd probably just hire him and pay weekly as he performs the work. But bear in mind that your deck could be half built when your tenant gets a job promotion or family emergency elsewhere and has to leave or no longer has extra time. Unfortunately, the hiring of tenants, and even work/ trade agreements with them, are never as black and white as they are with workers in the real world.

"Anybody Else?"

Even if applicants have already answered this question on the phone, verify in person: "Now, exactly who will be in your household?"

"Oh, just me, my husband, and our seventeen-year-old son."

Seems reasonable. But a seasoned landlady will ruminate, "Seventeen, hm, probably has a bunch of teenage friends.... And will he be getting a vehicle?"

Keep chatting to see what else gets coughed up. Keep asking, "Anybody else?" This question is easier by phone than in person, because it can be hard to keep a straight face at their answers.

A commonplace story on Kaua'i is large extended families living in closer quarters than most Mainlanders are accustomed to. I'd frequently get calls from more than seven full-grown people wanting to share my three-bedroom/one-bath unit. And though a cultural norm and possibly heaps of fun, it was overload for my place. Yes, they're congenial; yes, they're hardworking; yes, they'll pay the rent every month (1/7th each comes to almost nothing); yes, they're all about family; yes, they go to bed early and get up early; and no, they don't drink. You may believe you're getting easygoing, no-problem folk, because the families are so grateful you took them that they'll never bother you about anything ever! But do you really want seven showers taken every day, your toilet flushing nonstop, your washer spinning constantly, extra cars parked all over the lawn? Plus all their friends and relatives popping in, or moving here from the Philippines? You probably wouldn't even realize if a few more moved in.

And when these tenants eventually vacate, you'll see what all that wear and tear did to your sweet little spot.

But if you're not finding anybody suitable, stay cool. As far as renters know, you've got qualified candidates lining up. Don't reveal urgency, or exude sentiments like, "I really gotta get someone in here!" or, "I'm going nuts! I can't stand all these phone calls!"

For promising prospects, though, show the place quickly, "I'll be showing it later today, if you're available to come by." If they're not free, say, "I'm also showing it tomorrow." This implies you have lots of appointments.

And keep your vacant unit ready to show (not pristine necessarily, but presentable), so in a pinch, you can get there ten minutes before the appointment and tidy up. You can always say, "Excuse the slight disarray, we're doing some touch-ups while it's empty."

A fairly common occurrence can be one individual viewing the property, who would now like their other half to see it. Here, you'd say, "If you're seriously interested, try to get your spouse to come soon since I have other interested parties. Unfortunately, I can't hold the place for anyone." You don't say, "Well, if you want it, you better grab it because I can't sit around waiting."

"Well, can you hold it for the rest of the day?" she might ask.

"If your husband wants to come later today or tomorrow morning, I'm willing to do that," you could say. But know that there's a decent chance it won't work out anyway because, for some unknown reason, humans don't seem to appreciate when someone accommodates them. Just explain that you must continue showing the place because, until money changes hands, there's no legal agreement. *Always keep your application process moving along.* If someone's keen on your rental, you won't have to chase them.

If someone wants you to halt your process while they fumble around, usually looking at other places, the following statement will wake them up. "If you like the place and I approve of you, then you'd have to be ready to give me earnest money—a *nonrefundable* cash deposit of, say $400, toward your first month's rent. And I'd give you a receipt stating I have that money and that we'll do the lease signing in the next day or two."

When the woman then looks at you, "What? Why would we give you $400 cash in advance?" this only shows she's not very serious.

"Because I can't make a one-way commitment."

"Not even for *one day*?" she's already starting to hate you.

"The deposit is what tells me you're serious."

Realistic renters know how the process works. If you have to explain, then this space opera is usually at the finale. You need people ready to plunk down the deposit, so everyone can move forward.

More often than not, the squeaky wheel will get the grease—tenants who not only want it, not only like it, but need it. And hopefully, they're candidates you believe will work out for you.

Finally, don't bother trying to line up tenants in advance. If your unit will be vacant April 1st, don't try to set up your next tenants in February, or even early March. You're usually wasting energy. There are always people who don't need to move yet and have time to scout around. Some don't have to move at all but always keep an eye out for something better than what they have. Unless what you're offering is superior to most of what's out there, these looky-loos will rarely become your tenants. But if someone suitable truly wants it in advance, collect at least the first month's rent (nonrefundable) as soon as possible, and get the lease signed asap.

But this scenario gets clumsy if the applicants are an ocean away—requesting all kinds of photos and validation from you, then being wildly resistant about sending any money. "We can't just send you money without ever meeting you or seeing the place! You know how many scammers are out there?"

"I do. That's why this probably won't work out," I learned to state right up front. "But the only way you can secure the rental is to send money. So you have to seriously consider that before we spend more time discussing everything. So I'll let you get back to me."

15

Things to Keep in Mind

New to the Island

A big demographic on Kaua'i is the steady stream of new arrivals from the U.S. Mainland. Generalizing, they could be described as a) knowing little about either the island, the State of Hawai'i, or island dwelling, and b) needing a landing place from day one, to avoid the expense of a hotel and to establish an address to ship their possessions to.

Everyone knows that finding a decent rental in advance, sight-unseen, is beyond risky. So island-bound house hunters surf the web for something as short-term and reasonably priced as possible, just to secure a landing pad. And even before booking their flights, their dinner table conversation probably went like this:

Spouse #1, "Let's just get a place to start off, then once we're settled, we'll look around for either the house we want to buy or land to build on, or even a rental we just love. We can't possibly do that on line from here in Chattanooga. So let's just nail down something for our arrival, then take it from there."

Spouse #2, "Right, cuz once we're on the island, it's gonna take time to decide exactly where we'll want to live. Especially if we're buying something. But honey, we'll probably have to sign a lease…."

Spouse #1, "Well, we can get out of the lease when we need to. And if not, then we can just sublet it or something. But we shouldn't worry about that—we'll get the shortest lease we can."

Spouse #2, "Okay, Fun Buns, you're the brilliant one."

Starry-eyed and gung-ho, they touch down in Aloha Land. They've got money and exuberance, while little un-assuming you has no awareness that they just need base camp to commence their search.

You innocently sign them on. But before even sleeping off their jet lag, they're sniffing around for their jungle fantasy or beachfront shack. (Amazing how many people believe there are "shacks" on the beach here, sitting empty, that they can rent or even buy for peanuts. I've had to enlighten numerous newbies, "Believe me, anyone with oceanfront property on Kaua'i knows its worth.")

The real problem in seeking real estate in any hot market is that when you find something desirable, you have to jump. Maybe in West Virginia you can say, "I'll be back tomorrow to show it to my wife," but not in Hawai'i. So your three-week-old tenants now come sniveling, "We're really sorry but we have to move out. *We're buying a house!* Isn't that fantastic?! We're so excited! Can you work with us?"

Handle this however you like. But their objective is to wiggle out of the lease and recoup every possible nickel. You can "work with them," if their idea of work is akin to what Scott the Bomb, arranged—a win-win: he's cut free from the lease and I get a month and a half extra rent and a new bed. But in tenant-speak, "work with us" more likely means, "let us off the hook and you take the hit." Because *obtaining their landing pad* was crucial and they were kissing your feet, while *dumping you* to get on with their agenda is a mere hindrance. C'mon, they're manifesting their true destiny, the last thing they want clouding their ecstasy is your lease around their necks. "Where's the aloha?" they accuse. "We thought this was Paradise."

"It was Paradise 'til you got here."

But no matter how staunchly you defend the bylaws of what they signed, you're just a coldhearted gouger. Or "a greedy grubber," as Trisha called me. (See chapter 20, entitled "Trisha.")

But with most Hawai'i landlords seeking long-term renters, and hotels pricey, numerous flush newcomers have little choice but to sign a six-month or one-year lease, even when they know they'll be breaking it. And not knowing how long their "real home" quest will take, they must keep their mission secret from their new landlord.

Unfortunately for you, lease breaking is too run-of-the-mill for judges to get their knickers in a knot over. As long as rent was paid for the weeks or months of actual residence, you don't have a court case. And some newcomers have been landlords themselves and know that leases can be broken with little to no legal consequence.

I had one guy named Rich, who, before even unpacking, got a better job on O'ahu and moved over there, dragging his wife away with him, though she didn't want to go. (Her work, curiously, was commuting to Alaska two weeks per month, to clean apartments of oil rig guys.)

The wife had arrived on Kaua'i two months earlier, was extremely pleasant, and had excitedly set up the household. But she now gave in to her husband, and they took off.

As a pawn in their game, I guess, though more seasoned by then, I held my ground.

"You said you would work with us!" Rich grew heated on the phone.

"'Working' with you would mean *negotiating* about your breaking the lease. All you're saying is that you already left and you want a refund. That's not negotiation. What are you offering me?"

He became furious, "You said you would work with us, and now you're not prepared to do anything at all!" Thankfully, Rich was calling from O'ahu, not down the road…because he was forceful.

"You broke the lease and walked out. That has nothing to do with me. It's always going to cost money to do that sort of thing." *LESSON :* Tenants can and will break leases. And though it's against the terms of the agreement and in conflict with the landlord/tenant codes in every municipality, breaking a lease is not technically *illegal*. Not on Kaua'i, anyway. And should it get to court, you'll almost never win. Why? Lease breaking is commonplace. There are endless reasons why people break them—some good, some fake, some ridiculous. But all the judge cares about (I speak from experience) is, "Did you receive rent money for the time the tenant dwelled in your unit?"

Because, for judges, trying to decipher fact from fiction, as to *why* someone broke a lease, is nearly impossible. Were the tenants' parents really both killed in a plane crash, leaving these grieving renters solely responsible for the family ranch in North Dakota? And did this inhumane slob of a landlord really expect the tenants to still honor the full term of their Kaua'i lease at a tragic interlude like this?

Meanwhile, can a *landlord* break a lease with some far-flung excuse? Ha! Landlords can't even break the lease if they sell the property. They can't even break it if they die!

Cheerier news is that most renters *believe* leases are legally binding. (And don't alert them otherwise.) Or at least they want their security deposit back. So just be clear-in-the-head that the security deposit is your power, not the lease. Leases can be shockingly weightless in a court of law.

Ultimately, to safeguard not getting stuck with renters I was unhappy with, I'd start with only a six-month lease, saying we could probably extend if both parties wanted to. This is protective for landlords on two counts, because when tenants are hoping to extend, that shorter lease also keeps them behaving.

Long-term?

In my observation, most landlords and property managers will simply meet a bunch of applicants, check credit scores and call references, then select someone based on statistical criteria like good jobs and good credit. Most are chiefly about the bottom line and have a more hands-off approach than I. "Get good tenants in there and keep 'em as long as possible. Leave 'em alone and bank the dough."

These landlords don't like turnover. They don't want fuss. Wear and tear is expected, and they don't mind forking out a few grand to fully re-paint their units when long-termers eventually leave. They expect and accept expenditures like new stoves and refrigerators.

Sure, rent checks are steadier with long-term renters, but these dwellers also leave their massive couch on your newly finished living room floor for five years. They'll never accept having no wall decorations, so you probably have to permit it—meaning you'll have to repaint every room. And they won't clean the oven because, "Of course she's gonna buy a new stove when we leave, we've been here five years!" While short-termers hardly use the oven.

Long-term renters are seeking a "home" to make their own, and to my way of thinking, get too comfortable. There's no way someone won't become proprietary about a place they've lived in for years. They begin to feel it's theirs, not yours. With barnacle tenants, you can never get in to do a deep clean, and everything in the unit gets stale, the backs of the cupboards are full of old rice. And even if you inspect once a year (you must), you won't get to the heart of the matter. You might even begin to feel awkward conducting inspections, as if you're intruding in their space. Feels rude rummaging through their closets and cabinets to check for roaches, or to see how clean they are. So you may even become lax about inspecting.

But you must inspect. Even if you don't think it's necessary. Inspection is how you take a reading. You need to know what's going on in the unit because, as a landlord, you learn that sometimes little meets the eye.… Like you might open the bathroom medicine cabinet to observe some telling quantity of pills. I'm not saying pry into their personal lives, but shelf upon shelf of prescription drugs might give you pause. (But don't say, "Geez Louise, I had no idea your health was in crisis!")

Also, houses require continuous upkeep. If you're not up to date with thorough inspections, you can be unaware of plumbing drips or leaks, mold from a season of heavy rainfall (tropical reality), electric fixtures on the blink, or things that are disintegrating—issues tenants don't mention, for fear you'll charge them for the repair.

Long-standing tenants also gain an unspoken kind of leverage, "Well, we've been here so long...." where you're expected to sort of leave them alone. "Y'know, we've been really good tenants, we've paid our rent for three years now. Y'know, you took that trip and you didn't have to worry about us...." Trade-offs or friendliness or favors can all add up to you losing your power and even control.

LESSON : This will sound rough, but *you don't want tenants to have leverage.* That's why you don't have them over for pizza. You *can't.* Give them a centimeter, they'll take an acre.

So I generally steered away from long-term. And yes, I diverged from the landlord flock in that I was more territorial, call it picky, about my property. But transient types have a lighter footprint, are less apt to cart in Matson-loads of clunky furniture and art for every wall. They may have one car instead of two, their children may be off on the Mainland somewhere. As long as they stay four to six months, I don't mind transients. And you can always renew decent short-term tenants.

Believe it or not, and you probably won't, but I *never once in sixteen years* had to re-paint my interior walls between tenants. Because it stated in my lease that tenants couldn't put holes in the walls for any reason, and if they did, the cost of repainting that entire room would come out of their deposit. I'd explain simply, "For a short-term rental like this, I can't allow it. I'm sure you understand."

And you can state the same. Short-term renters understand that logic.

And there are droves of short-termers out there—from people with temp jobs, to people saving up money to buy a home, to people building a house over yonder rise, to traveling nurses, to people who just got divorced and somebody has to move, to…you name it.

Also, in my opinion, it's way easier to have a professional cleaner (or yourself) spruce up the place once or twice a year for $200, than to have a team of painters raging through for thousands, while you scramble around cleaning up behind them.

Short-term always provides you an out clause, too. Granted, you have to interview more often, write out more leases, and adjust to new personalities and foibles, but the property will at least feel like *yours*.

Again though, most landlords go for long-term renters followed by painting squads.

My penultimate set of tenants, a family from Mexico who'd been in the US a number of years, wanted to stay-stay-stay whenever their lease expired. Breaking my pattern —partly because the guy was pretty nice and partly because I was getting lazier by the end of my landlord tenure—and despite the wife's dour demeanor and them lying about not having a dog—I continued renewing them. When they finally left after two and a half years, the damage to that unit cost me thousands. They destroyed the wood flooring by putting urine pads down for their unpermitted pooch. And the cockroach situation in the kitchen and bathroom was so cringe-worthy, I had to restore the entire bathroom.

Because I had the massive and costly undertaking of refinishing the wood floors throughout the house, they didn't get their deposit back, making the mother even surlier.

"I'm going to call my lawyer," threatened the guy, when I delivered the bad news about the deposit, complete with documents, labor receipts, and photos.

"Do whatever you want," I was unfazed. "Would you like copies of all this documentation?"

"No!" (That was revealing, since lawyers always require paperwork). But these customers KNEW they'd destroyed the floors and left a roach infestation. And this CAN occur with long-term renters, while no one can breed a multi-generational roach colony in only six months.

Profiling

On Craigslist, from which I drew tenants, there's a policy about not "profiling." Landlords aren't allowed to discriminate. But Craigslist's "discrimination" is actually laughable (or just lip service), because who's not going to discriminate about who lives on their property? Choosing the best tenant, i.e. protecting yourself and your investment, isn't discrimination, but common sense. So no matter how p.c. some might wish the world to be, landlords will rent to whomever they please.

But some feisty applicant might bring this up, some dweeb asserting their "rights," "You can't tell me I can't have a dog because it's a service dog."

Guess what, hon, my decision has to do with *you* and your entitlement issues, not the sweet dog. But you don't say that, you just calmly reply, "Yes, I know. I totally understand that's the law. So let me get back to you as soon as I go through all my applications." The fact is, even if legally we have to permit the support creature, we don't have to permit its owner. Rent to whomever you please. You have to be discriminatory and select the best possible candidates. Just don't discuss your selection process with applicants.

Drinkers

Due to the belligerence, arguments, partying, and odious behavior that can accompany seasoned drinkers, I grew to zero tolerance for them in my rentals. *LESSON:* If you take no other guidance from this book, at least let the next sentence sink in: Alcohol is a landlord's worst enemy.

Seek to determine if applicants are drinkers. Whether they drink every day is a reasonable guideline. But asking them outright is ill-advised because, aside from offending and maddening them, you risk being reported to Craigslist for discrimination. Then your ad will be removed.

But during the interview process, I'd ofttimes couch the topic as a throwaway remark maybe ten minutes into our sit-down interview, "So, you mentioned that you guys don't smoke, what about drinking? You guys drink at all?"

They might say yes, thinking you're about to offer them a beer.

Don't appear judgmental, though. Never tell applicants you don't want drinkers! If pressed, just assert, with a toothy grin, "Oh, I never tell anybody how they should live! I just had a negative experience once with an excessive drinker, so I'm a little careful. I'm sure you understand." But everything hinges on their responses to comments like that. In fact, this benign session could come to an abrupt halt.

Why is this issue so grave? Well, it's no secret that alcoholics aren't the world's peacemakers. For landlords, though, the concern is that tenants can't be evicted for alcoholic behavior because it's legal to drink in one's own home. And it's kind of a bummer when you're the one who owns that horrible house where the tenants are driving the whole neighborhood bonkers. Should you get caught up in this, you'll find out—possibly by the police, like I did—that it's legal in Hawai'i to hang out in one's yard drinking, even with all one's friends, any time between 7 a.m. and 10 p.m. It's even legal to make outrageous noise while so doing. But believe me, you won't be smiled upon when telling your kindly neighbors that they only have to wait ten more months for the partying to subside. Yet there's *nothing a landlord can do* except explain to these seething neighbors that your hands are tied because drinking in one's own yard is legal.

So if an applicant asks you in astonishment, "Are you saying that we can't have a drink in our own home?" just gently and discreetly wind down the interview.

Tell them you've got several other people to consider and you'll be in touch. Then part with, "Give me a few days, and if you don't hear from me, feel free to give a call."

On the other hand, applicants may reply, "Oh no, no, we're church people."

Yay! Boom, you're done! Church people are rarely drunks.

But they could also say something like, "Well, we're not like teetotalers, we don't sit around with apple cider, but we're working people, y'know, we're busy. We go to bed at 8:30, get up, and go to work." And that's a positive response, because hardcore drinkers rarely hit the hay at 8:30.

Or perhaps the wife will say, "Well, Josh watches football on Sundays with the guys and they usually have some beers."

"Kinda like a weekly ritual?" you might nudge.

"Oh, he wishes it was a weekly ritual, but he's the head of a construction crew so he gets up at 5:30 every morning and works his butt off. And Sundays are our only family day."

Any man working that hard to care for a family gets my vote and often my lease.

Bear in mind, though, that serious drinkers don't identify as "serious drinkers," but as "social drinkers." And I've had tenants say they're sober as monks, then watched Coors Light cans fill their recycling bin month after month.

So someone might say, "I mean, we have wine with dinner, but we don't, like, *drink*." And where an AA member thinks "wine with dinner" means a drinker, this applicant thinks, 'It's only wine, for cripe sake!'

It can be abstruse. But if s/he phrases it, "We'll have a glass of wine with dinner every now and then, or if we're celebrating something," that's less ambiguous.

Just tread lightly. If they squint at you when you mention drinking, "You're getting a little too personal here...." or they're tipsy from a champagne brunch, take your cue and cross them off. You can't risk it.

What might come your way if you take drinkers? You can't even imagine.

Tenants on the Same Property

Many landlords have one or more rental units on the property where they reside. Frequently that's their only option—inherited properties, or just the layout of what they own. If you have the choice—i.e. haven't yet purchased a rental property—it's not the optimal arrangement. Especially if you're a single female. Not that tenants are dangerous, just that you'll have no moral support, no buffer, and less privacy when sharing the same turf.

You want sanctuary where you live. You don't want to come home to "work." I personally would rather not even think about my tenants unless I'm *thinking about my tenants* due to a situation in progress. I don't want to enter my own driveway to discover my tenants have guests from the Mainland or got a Great Dane. I want to have a bite and watch my reality show. I don't want to hear them clumping around upstairs or scolding their kids. Or wonder why someone drove in or out at 3 a.m.

With tenants sharing your space, their whole lifestyle, for better or worse, is in your face. Plus yours is open to them—your comings and goings, friends and lovers, relations, habits, guests, even your purchases and possessions, even occasional unrest in your life...like that stoned brother. ("You travel all the time. You must have a lot of money. So, why are you raising our rent?") And are you okay with them seeing you in your pajamas?

No matter how congenial tenants are or seem, no matter how good your relationship starts out or even stays, the hierarchy is unspoken and ever present. If you're lucky, tenants respect it and want to be in your good graces. If not, resentment can simmer, even boil over. And should there be any form of conflict, do you want that brewing right where you water your plants and let your animals play?

Maybe I'm just squeamish or maybe I overly cherish my solitude and peace, but as a single woman living alone, I'm protective about my personal life, especially in these wacky and uncertain times.

LESSON : If your set-up involves sharing the same property with tenants, you may want to initially offer lower rent to attract a high number of applicants to choose from. Then select the very best. A working middle-aged woman is a savvy choice. And start with a month-to-month or six-month lease to see how things play out.

Bending Rules

Some units are easier to rent than others. My back unit was off the street, with ample and quiet yard, thus something of a love nest. As long as I accurately priced it, it was a breeze to find qualified takers, and tenants were always content. I even let one or two good ones stay several years. And I also lived there twice myself and loved it.

If you have, in fact, experienced a unit yourself, even for a month or two, that makes listing its attributes and features much easier. "It's silent here at night because it's off the street, there are no barking dogs, the elderly back neighbors are kindly and keep to themselves, you can't see through the foliage so you have total privacy, and nobody ever comes back here." In any tight market, it's imperative to know the pluses of what you're offering. You can also address the neighborhood, "This neighborhood may not look too posh, but it's all families, totally safe, and actually a great place to live. And it's a very mixed demographic, and central on the island." I would add, "It's also a cul-de-sac, so there's no through traffic. The only cars are people going to work in the morning and coming home at the end of the day. Otherwise, it's totally mellow."

But second (and third and fourth) units are known for rule bending, even being totally illegal, i.e. bootlegged. In my back kitchen, I took the risk of installing a bigger sink than permitted and the countertop was ten feet instead of the coded six. I figured I'd rework it if raided by the Kitchen Police, though I didn't dare put in a stove. But I remember asking Carter, my realtor (the slumlord with twenty-one units that were making him rich), about it all. And he casually replied, "If they shut you down, they gotta shut down the whole town, because every house on that part of the island has at least one back unit, some three or four. They're never gonna crack down on everybody." Indeed, mayhem would've ensued. So extra units were all but grandfathered in. But don't bend rules too far. Because when some scrappy tenant rats you out, it can ruin your day.

Fortunately, that kitchen was unusually spacious and attractive, so renters never cared about its limitations, like no oven. And younger people didn't need an oven because they don't cook, so the double hot plate and microwave sufficed just fine.

Litigation

When breaking leases, my more levelheaded tenants acknowledged that *they* were breaking the lease and *I* shouldn't have to bear responsibility. While others fought to get their full deposits back, with no remorse about leaving me high and dry. There are also incorrigible chumps out there who work the angles every time they rent a place. And should you find yourself IN their angle, you'll get worked.

Unfortunately, I'm a lousy candidate to run one's game on. Though I'm fair, sensitive, and understanding, I have low tolerance for BS and am no fan of one-way commitments. (As if a *landlord* could ever simply break a lease because of a divorce or a sick parent on the Mainland.)

But take note, this isn't the same as "pick your battles," because landlords can't *have* battles. And in the course of my sixteen and a half years, I lost my temper maybe once. Maybe never. YOU HAVE TO keep a lid on it—they're living on your property! They can really harm the place, or even you (physically and/or emotionally). By their attitude and remarks alone, they can make your life miserable. Or by what they say *about* you, or even by slander (saying false things about you). And they will, should you give them perceived cause to "get even." *LESSON :* Never challenge your tenants, never confront them directly with the slightest aggression or anger.

You *can* sue for slander, btw...but hold your horses. Most landlords will warn you not to entertain litigation as a recourse or winning tactic. Even by threatening litigation, you're declaring war on your tenants, who, remember, live on *your* property. So don't be trigger-happy.

And lawsuits are time consuming, complicated, expensive, and a crapshoot. The judge can decide against you even if you're certain you were right. Landlord/tenant cases can also be loaded against landlords, because the general public—should you have a jury—as a rule, regards tenants as working class underdogs and landlords as rich gaugers. True or untrue, fair or unfair, that's kind of where it's at. Though you won't hear anyone but landlords ever say it.

How then do you handle confrontational developments?

If you're clever—and you are now, being more than halfway through this book—you'll tell tenants up front, and right in the beginning, when you think or hope they're lovely people, "I go by the book. I'm well acquainted with the landlord/tenant rulebook and I adhere to it." That way, nothing is an emotional issue or what you "feel." If the tension doesn't ease up, simply reiterate, "In terms of what's expected from you, I go by the rulebook of the State of Hawai'i. Most everything is spelled out there. The rules work nicely when everybody follows them." For emphasis, you can fan yourself with that slim paperback. Or fan yourself with this one, it's thicker.

Also, before they signed the lease, I would say, "Read the entire lease carefully. I want you to read it in full and understand what you're signing."

If, mournfully, you do end up in court, just do your absolute best, with the most competent paid or unpaid advice and support you can scare up. If you're a senior, there may be free services available. Just remember that each state is different, so adhere like the dickens to regional laws.

16

Lease Details

The Lease

There are a variety of leases out there—some rudimentary or short, some long and involved, some riddled with legalese no one understands, some just poorly written. You want a succinct, easy to read lease, neither suspiciously short nor annoyingly long, that is pro-landlord and covers *your derriere*. By pro-landlord, I don't mean unfairly so, just not slanted in tenants' favor.

The first one I used didn't protect me enough, nor have all the significant points itemized. My second one, donated by Carter, and I believe created by a realtor association, I used for all the years to follow. It was four full pages, two of which spelled out everything both tenants and landlords could and couldn't do. *LESSON :* You need a pro-landlord lease. Other landlords or realtors or property managers can help you find a good one.

Make sure to acquire a lease that's legally accurate, clear, all-encompassing, and concise. Because in a courtroom, the verdict usually, not always, comes down to what's stated therein. Anything not in writing can be dismissed by a judge as "he said/she said." But if your lease says they can't put holes in the wall, not even one little nail—and they signed it, that's tangible.

Fear not, new tenants won't scrutinize the verbiage of your lease. For applicants wanting or needing the unit, this is no time to dicker over semantics. Even when they read it over in detail, most will just figure, "Hey, it looks official." Few of us sign enough leases in a lifetime to know what should or shouldn't be included, how long it should be, or whose favor it's in. Truth is, other than vintage landlords, scammers, property managers, and real estate attorneys, no one's well-versed in the ins and outs of landlord/tenant law.

LESSON : Convey to all tenants that this lease, these pages we're signing are for real. "Read them carefully and abide by them, and we'll be fine."

But be aware there are shabby shysters working the system, who, no matter what the lease says, know the loopholes before even answering your ad.

The Addendum

You can add to your lease anything you deem important or any "house rules" you wish to attach. On day one, I created an addendum page that I stapled to the lease and had new tenants initial every item listed there.

These were largely issues not mentioned in the lease, such as a) assigned parking spots for each unit; b) that they could only plant things in pots, not in the ground; c) that they couldn't store anything on the property (boats, furniture, old cars, etc.); d) that when they moved out, they must remove all their effects; e) that they couldn't leave their excess trash or recycling in the carport or elsewhere when they vacated; and f) that they must have their mail forwarded through the post office when they left, "Landlord will not be responsible for forwarding mail."

In an addendum, you can itemize any expectations you wish, even reiterating things already in the lease that might need underscoring. Like, "Only people listed as tenants may live in the house. You may not have anyone else staying in the house without landlord's express permission." By requiring them to initial this point, you know they've now read it twice.

The Yard

In addition to the gardener's regular visits, keep your yard up to snuff. It's more important than you'd think.

An unsightly mess outside is unacceptable. But it can happen. And quickly. I never had that trial for even a day because I wrote into every lease that, aside from a biweekly gardener who'd mow and weed-whack, paid for by tenants but hired by me, I myself would handle the pruning and weeding. I knew from the start that if I left lawn maintenance to tenants, a) the yard would be unattended, messy, and shaggy, b) I'd always be irritated, and c) I'd lose both access to and control over the property.

Also, in today's reality, "gardeners" only mow, blow, and go. So if you want things blooming and happy, that effort has to be orchestrated separately. Easiest to handle yourself. (And your foliage needn't be eye-popping—simple and basic is fine.)

Having that personal access not only kept everything groomed, but gave me surveillance. Because at any time, seven days a week, 9 a.m. to 5 p.m., I could pop by, shears in hand. And since, obviously, I was caretaker of the yard, this arrangement spared me having to press tenants to remove rain-soaked sofas and bins of unrecycled cans.

When you maintain the grounds, a) you have easy access to the property; b) everything stays trimmed and clean; c) you remain up to date about what's going on there; and d) you set a high standard for how things should look, and tenants know you care. But remember, you're *gardening*, not pretending to garden while snoopin' around. (But I always, privately, asked my gardener to keep an eye out for any peculiarities at the property. Like, someone's mother sitting on the porch…. Has she moved in?)

"Why can't we take care of the yard ourselves?" new tenants would invariably ask.

"You're going to be really happy that someone else handles it," I'd explain, with absolute certainty. "Things grow really fast here, but you'll never have to come home and say, 'Oh God, we have to mow.' Your yard will always look nice, and you'll never have to think about it. Plus you won't have to labor in the hot sun, or buy and store a lawnmower, Weedwacker, leaf-blower, and gas container. And since there are two units, you get to split the gardener cost. It's also good for me because I don't have to worry about whether you're keeping up with it, or fret if everything gets overgrown. It's totally worthwhile and much easier for everybody. Plus, I have a great, reliable, and inexpensive gardener."

Who could say no to that?

LESSON: Keep personal control over the yard.

Also, since "growing food" is part of The Garden Island dream life people are "manifesting," testing one's horticultural acumen is as common as trying to surf. But, although the notion of a vegetable garden is thrilling, few have a green thumb, agricultural aptitude, time to garden, or money for pots, soil, and tools. And almost without exception, tenants were too busy and consumed by devices to ever even venture outdoors, let alone tend herbs or install chicken wire around their cherry tomatoes. They never even watered during droughts.

Ergo, I recommend writing into your addendum, "Any outdoor planting must be in pots only or in raised beds." Because once tenants have vacated, you don't need a patchwork lawn with dried out eggplant or cilantro gone to seed.

In your addendum, also include "no parking on the grass." Kaua'i people adore parking on grass, especially right next to ample paved parking…something about not letting four-wheel-drive go to waste, or not wanting to lug their beer cooler an extra twenty feet. "It's a local thing," a haole acquaintance of mine condescended.

Oh, okay then, it's *cultural*!

Just create a nice lawn and work to keep it that way.

Rare Leniency

Briefly, on the subject of security deposits…. Though you can never be lax in collecting it in full, it is the one grey area during the move-in process where you *may* offer tenants some breathing room. Not advised as standard practice, but let's say their payday isn't until next week and money's tight due to the move. You could, conceivably, give them an extra week to submit the balance of the deposit. Like, "Two thirds now and one third next Wednesday, when you get paid." Or half and half. Only on rare occasions and when I felt certain they'd comply, did I accommodate new tenants this way, to take some stress out of their move. But you must clearly state, "This is a one-time concession—since it's not the rent, but the deposit—and I know you're good for it." But notate it in writing, to the penny, have them sign it, and collect the money on the agreed-upon day.

Part IV

Wising Up

≡ *17* ≡

Couples

A lot of newly formed couples think, "Hey, you're hot, I'm hot, let's live together. We'll cozy up and save some money." They get "new couple" status, plus twice the space they could afford solo.

But shucks, suddenly they're not getting along. Then someone either storms out or gets asked to leave. In survival mode now, they start scrambling. Then they officially call it quits and one is left holding the lease.

LESSON : Unless something about an unmarried pair boldly spells "lock-step for the long-term," break-ups can happen. Married people on the other hand, despite their differences, probably won't pull the plug on your watch.

When break-ups occur, guess who's the last to know. And all the couple wants from you, once you get the memo, is bending and accommodating. Because it wasn't their fault—terrible things happen in life! You should *weep about their misfortune* and make every possible concession.

The surviving tenant's Plan A will be to request a rent discount, "because obviously I can't pay the full rent by myself." But having expected your unfavorable reaction to that, Plan B is, "Well, I guess I either have to break the lease or get a new housemate."

The reason why *you've* become the fall guy is obvious to judges: It was your mistake renting to an unmarried couple. And of course you can't collect the full rent from someone who truly doesn't have the means to pay it. "As a landlord, you should know better," is what it comes down to.

And, were you to pursue your "right" to hold them to the lease, the court would commonly side with the tenant—despite the lease, addendum, and any verbal warnings you claim to have issued before lease signing. So your choices now are simple: either release both star-crossed lovers or permit Surviving Tenant to get a new housemate.

My first schooling on this came from Greg and Sandy, an unmarried pair who split up after just a few months. In no time flat, Sandy was gone.

But Greg, a peach actually, decided to keep the place, live up to his lease, and get on with his productive life. Manager of a sizable construction company, he had integrity and enough money. He didn't feel like moving again, and my house was close to his worksite.

Actually another of my best tenants, Greg ended up staying three whole years, with nothing but good vibes. He even helped me with a giant plumbing issue by bringing his construction crew to the house on a Sunday, to dig up the whole front yard so we could redo the pipes. And didn't charge me!

It was a cryin' shame when Greg got transferred back to the Mainland.

But though I lucked out with him, that wasn't the case with the next experimental family unit: arrogant young Briana, her small son, and her scroungy Hyundai salesman, who rapidly went AWOL.

Briana then claimed abandonment and blanket injustice from…the world at large. How can you possibly expect me to come up with the rent, you insensitive capitalist?

That first month, her mother came through with mercy funding. "I feel so sorry for my daughter. She had this relationship and he turned out to be a two-timer. He lied, he cheated, he didn't pay the rent. And now my poor daughter and her little son are left to fend for themselves!"

But demon seed Briana, who'd somehow bagged an unsuspecting co-pay for one fleeting moment, couldn't remotely fend for herself. And I, living in the back unit at the time, was now the Dragon Lady lacking all compassion.

As it played out, Briana's entitlement complex was so inflated that, just to breathe freely, I had to cut her loose. But I also had to abide her time-frame as she supposedly searched for another place…until finally, after a month of her pouting, Mommy took the little millennial back home.

But beware, if there's one thing as bad as a bad tenant, it's Bad Tenant's mother. And had those two dragged me to the courthouse, they'd surely have won. Possibly just by Briana being a voluptuous young woman, but also by her lying and having Mommy on hand orating the Shakespearian misfortune of it all and the Dragon Lady's heartlessness. "He said/*they* said" holds more sway with judges than "he said/*she* said."

Because I let Briana off, we didn't go to court. But I was to learn later that a lease only holds up in court *in relation to circumstance.* A judge will ask a landlord outright, "Did you talk to her about it? Were you reasonable with her? Did you acknowledge her hardship and accommodate her circumstances in any way?"

Even with a signed clause reading, "If either one of the couple vacates the unit before the term of the lease, the other is solely responsible for the rent," a judge will almost never hold Surviving Tenant liable.

But had I replied to the judge, "Well, Your Honor, I didn't want her to get some low-life alternate roommate," the judge would've probably had the bailiff escort me from the chamber.

It comes down to money. Everyone knows the young, single woman can't bear a financial blow, while the piggy landlord can. So judges and juries are predictably more sympathetic to tenants. Call it what you will. (And you didn't hear it from me.)

I now posit that renting to unmarried couples requires a disclaimer. After Briana, I'd always clarify with couples, "Because you're not married, only one of you will take responsibility for this rental. Because if you break up, you can't come and say, 'Oh, we broke up, and the one who's staying can't afford it alone.' So only one will be the actual leaseholder, and the other will be listed on the lease as a resident. But should you separate, Surviving Tenant can't just haul in some willy-nilly new roomie. Any new person has to be vetted and approved by me."

"Yeah, yeah, no problem. But we're not gonna break up." And one of them will usually step up, "I don't mind, I'll take the responsibility, and we'll work out the details between us." Generally, one prefers having control anyway whilst the other's okay as a ride-along. But at least they heard you. And you must add a clause to your addendum: "If, for any reason, either _______ or _______ moves out, no one else may reside in the unit without express approval and permission from Landlord."

18

Shuffling and Adjusting

Raising the Rent

Obviously, you need to collect sufficient rent. But charging a slightly higher amount than before isn't always worth those few extra beans.

Raising rent is a timing thing. For instance, if you have solid existing tenants, you could lose them over a rent hike. And retaining time-tested tenants can save you tremendous fuss and aggravation. That extra $100 per month usually isn't worth disrupting the lives of decent people, plus having to start over with unknown entities. Even $200 extra may not be worth it.

Because when tenants vacate, the place is empty for a minimum of two weeks while you clean up and seek new renters—longer, if you're repairing or upgrading. And new renters frequently want to move in on the first of the next month, meaning you could even lose a whole month's rent. So, say you were charging $2000/month and now you're raising it to $2200. But you lose one month's rent ($2000) before your next tenants move in. It will now take you ten months, with that extra $200/month, to earn back the $2000 you lost for the empty month. So the entire next twelve months, you only gain an extra $200. You're better off keeping your great tenants another year, then letting them know, with plenty of lead time, that you'll be raising the rent the following year.

With rare exceptions, I only raised the rent between tenants.

But on occasions when you want or need to raise it, but wish to retain good tenants, then raise it only marginally. If you bump it up just $25-50 per month, to be split between two tenants with jobs, they hardly notice. Just make light of it, "I'm raising your rent, but only a little. It's going up only $40 a month. That's only $20 each, shouldn't be a problem." You'll still get $480 more per year. And with low numbers like that, you can even do it annually. Sometimes tenants will even express gratitude that you didn't raise it more.

On the other hand, upping the rent is an effective ploy for ousting tenants you're unhappy with. Instead of emoting that you won't renew their lease because you find them obnoxious and slovenly, you simply inform them—well in advance of their current lease ending—"Unfortunately, we have to raise the rent on this unit. As I told you when you moved in, the rent was unusually low due to the weak economy. But we're now bringing the price closer to what it's supposed to be." Or, "We're looking at some repairs coming up, and it's going to mean a modest rent increase."

Here though, if you only raise it $80/month, they'll probably stay anyway and just be more disrespectful. So the new amount has to be a deal-breaker. Their primary reason for renting your place was probably the bargain they got anyway, so they'll now likely scoot off in search of their next deal. And of course, once they're gone, you can charge your next tenants whatever amount you please.

During the recession that started in 2008 and lasted about seven years, everyone was hurtin' islandwide. Rents got lower and lower. At one point during that interim, my three-bedroom had been empty for five or six weeks. I kept reducing the rent, wondering how low I'd have to go. In an economic down trend, the way you determine what will stick is to start off high, then see who shows up. *LESSON :* If you need tenants and don't garner enough interest, lower your price.

On the other hand, unless your place is a dump, don't drop it so low that you're luring bottom feeders. People who nickel and dime their way through life, those who go catatonic over $50 more per month, may be penny-pinchers who question the electric bill every month, not trusting your accounting, and who go ape-shit over negligible hikes in the water bill. You don't want tightwads, nitpickers, or plain old cheapskates, unless you don't mind supplying them with monthly financial breakdowns. *LESSON :* People haggling over every dime will probably continue haggling over *every* dime.

Then they pull up in their shiny new Range Rover, "We got a great deal on it!"

Fixing and Replacing Things

Responsible renters alert you when the toilet isn't flushing right or the kitchen faucet leaks, so you or a professional can repair it. They don't let it drip, tape it up, or have Uncle Mickey monkey with it. And—unless these are picky tenants who text you about every dust-bunny—you, in normal landlord fashion, assure them you'll handle their concern in a timely manner. "Thank you for telling me. I'll come over and take a look at it this afternoon." Or if it's not urgent, "I appreciate your alerting me. I'll look into the solution and let you know in the next few days what's gonna happen and when."

You never say, "Really? What caused it? Did you mess with it? It was fine before." Just say, "Okay, tell me what you're experiencing. How long has it been happening? And what do you think the cause might be?" Many problems stem from basic wear and tear, but you do have to determine if tenants are misusing something. Like have they attached some gizmo to it?

If you're uncertain about what you're seeing or being told, a go-to resource can be the Home Depot or a friendly hardware store. There, at no charge, you can consult with employees. And if Joe in Aisle Twelve can't help, he'll send you to Sam in Aisle Five. Plus the parts they recommend are steps away. But it's guaranteed they'll use alien terminology and ask you for details, "How wide is the opening of the pipe?" or "Is it copper piping or galvanized?" So bringing a cell phone photo of your dilemma is highly recommended. But a store should be your initial resource, because handymen don't relish showering you with free advice. They prefer to just go fix it, for $100 just to start their truck.

Whomever you speak to, remember to ask, "What are my options?" Sometimes you have none, but sometimes several, including "Just clean the old one." Though restoring is hardly the American way, it's shocking how often cleaning something can spare you replacing it. Say it's a shower head through which water isn't properly flowing. A seventy-year-old handyman from Nebraska might tell you to run boiling water through it, or poke the holes with toothpicks, or boil it, or soak it in vinegar, or *whatever* he comes up with. Baking soda and vinegar cures crop up repeatedly.

Hopefully you have a handyman or skilled tradesman able to check things out. Otherwise, turn to Craigslist, YouTube, the Yellow Pages, or phone a realtor friend for references. Or by then you've become a handyman yourself and are thinking, "I know what this is and I know how to fix it." Bop over to Ace, pick up a toilet kit, and plunk it into their tank. Eventually you'll blow your own mind by how much you know. Lila (my helper) and I even put in a new dimmer light switch by ourselves.

Also, when something's broken, don't overlook the opportunity to upgrade. If you're paying a handyman to come over anyway, it can be worth a few more shekels for something more attractive or more efficient. Especially if you're planning to raise the rent soon, do some renovating, or sell the place. With lighting fixtures or towel racks, if you've got standard landlord cheapo types that've been there ten years, upgrading can't hurt, and tenants like when you improve their home at no extra charge. A minimal upgrade, though, shouldn't require repainting the whole bathroom because imprints from the old towel racks remained after the new ones were attached. (That's why seasoned landlords stick with the standardized fixtures that screw right back where the old ones came out.)

Also, don't be spendy on everyday items like drain strainers or appliances like stoves, refrigerators, and washing machines. Unless you've got an upscale unit, it's best to stay generic here because these things will need replacing more often than those in your own home.

Also, fix or upgrade *as troubles occur*, rather than waiting to tackle numerous issues at once when you finally have the time and money, or when the unit is empty. Because, piled up, repairs can really cost a bundle. Remember, too, that one thing may lead to another—water damage may lead to wood rot, or trim with paint flaking may indicate termite damage.

Another recommendation is to keep an extra set of doorknobs for each unit, to switch over each time tenants vacate. Though I didn't get this far myself, it would behoove you to learn doorknob installation. It's not overwhelming, only takes about fifteen minutes, and is something you'll pay someone to do over and over if you don't master it yourself. Plus the buying of new doorknobs all the time. Just keep an extra set for each unit, and swap them back and forth.

LESSON : Keep extra doorknob sets and learn how to change them. Instructions come in doorknob kits, or watch a tutorial.

Also, tenants will ask you for stuff—screen door, new hose, gravel in the driveway. Just say no and explain how it's fine, and you like it, the way it is. And make it clear they may not proceed on their own without your permission. Because if they do, it's promised to be executed poorly and cheaply.

On the other hand, if the request is justified or perhaps even a sound idea—legitimately time for a new hose, new shower head, new screens—check out the situation and tell them you'll take care of it.

Never let them handle it and send you the bill. It seems trite, but you can't risk anything. "Yeah, the new door sticks a little, but we don't mind! And we thought you'd be pleased we painted it to match the flowers by the porch." Or, "We figured a fifty-foot hose was fine, even though the old one was a hundred."

"Wean and Tean" vs. Abuse

"Normal wear and tear" is mentioned in leases. Expect and allow things like a funky shower curtain with mold along the bottom. And you can't charge the tenants. *LESSON :* Wear and tear happens—scuff marks on baseboards, dings in doorjambs and thresholds—from furniture being moved in and out.

And on the subject of doorjambs, there's no tenant on Earth who appreciates their worth. "Door what?" No one, except Californians, who stand in them during earthquakes, even knows what they are.

Doorjambs are simply the frame of a doorway. But for landlords, understanding their worth is 101. *LESSON :* Doorjambs must be protected because *they can't be replaced* (without extreme complication and expense). And they're in jeopardy every time tenants move in or out. Ditto for your wood flooring. (That's why almost no landlords have wood flooring.) And the cost of repairing a scratched wood floor, where that's even possible, can't be fathomed by the innocent renter with the guilty sofa. But discovering new scrapes or drag marks across your floor is ongoing, because furniture is continually moved around.

"What happened there?" is your legitimate question.

But don't expect, "Oh, we're so sorry. We got a new couch." Tenants NEVER cop to scrapes and gouges. Regarding the ding in the jamb or the gouge across the floor, they just stand there like sock puppets, "We didn't do that." Or they stare at you, "What's your problem, lady?" Or shrug. Or say, "I don't see anything" or, "That was already there" or, "We can fix it" or, "Oh, really? You think we did that?"

Sadly, there's *nothing* you can do about doorjamb damage, and next to nothing about wood floor scars. Just call your floor "distressed," and get on with your life. Because when you bust tenants about *anything*, especially with a hint of accusation, you'll get backlash. Everything translates to dollars in their minds, and they need their full deposit back to secure their next rental.

Moving In and Out

Since most dings and scrapes occur during moving, once I became proactive, I'd tell new tenants, "Getting a couch, or a big bed through that front door and inside those narrow porch railings is really challenging. So when you move in, you'll want a third person to coach the movers through that door. Cuz *I don't want dings in the doorjamb—* that thing right there." Then you say, "I'll try to stop by that day to see if maybe I can help out."

"No, I'm sure we'll be fine," they already don't want you around. And remember, they have the power now, you gave them the key. Or they'll say that their dad and uncle have lots of moving experience so you needn't fret.

You NEED fret. They won't mention that Dad and Uncle Ozzy drink twelve-packs to make the work more ~~careless~~ pleasant. Fret hard, then do whatever you must to avoid things dinging the jamb.

When tenants were moving into my rental, often I'd just casually show up, "I just wanted to see how the move is going. Need any help? I'm happy to grab some boxes." And unfailingly, there's not enough muscle, too much sun, too much furniture, or maybe raindrops, and a rented truck with its timer ticking. So even if you just grab a corner of a bed, it does help. Then I'd just stick around "helping," while discreetly protecting my house! Even just standing beside the two brutes wrangling that beastly bed through the front door will save you anguish. Because even "professional" movers (random strong young men willing to do manual labor) rarely take the necessary precautions.

Ditto, btw, for new refrigerators, stoves, dishwashers, washers, and dryers. One might assume delivery guys are trained in protecting doorjambs and flooring while wrestling appliances from their truck to your kitchen, but no. Nor do they welcome you dancing around hysterically. But stand your ground—in the doorjamb—and fight the good fight. Otherwise your jambs are doomed. At least with new appliances, it will be you, not the tenants, who ordered them, so your presence at delivery is required, thus won't annoy anyone. Here your fancy footwork will be in charming the movers enough that they'll let you spot them through the door and across the floor. Often they have a dolly, helping greatly, but sometimes they don't.

A groovy method I came up with years ago, for protecting hardwood floors from heavy things being dragged, is to use old moving mats—that I scored somewhere, and treasure to this day—or even a bunch of old towels. You place them across the threshold and into the room beforehand, and make sure they're thick enough. Then you instruct the movers to plunk the fridge onto your mats. Then they can just pull on the mats, and/or push the heavy item, and *slide* the whole mass across the floor. Works like a magic.

19

Good Tenants, Bad Tenants

During that recession, I was living in the back unit a second time and needed to fill the front. But due to limited responses and wondering about how far down I'd have to lower the rent, I was flustered. Money needed to flow in again, but islanders were struggling, moving back in with their parents, bitterly complaining, and even moving to the Ninth Island, also known as Las Vegas.

LESSON : Never be desperate!

An attractive young local woman showed up. She said she lived with her boyfriend of ten years and their two small children, and she worked part time as a waitress at a nearby resort. I can't recall what work she said her boyfriend did, but her answer passed muster. With her adorable five-year-old daughter in tow, the woman seemed on the level. And with little hesitation and few questions, she said she wanted the place, feeling everything about it suited her family needs and it was only a mile from her work.

I admit, in this instance, to judging a book by the cover; the woman was polite, nicely dressed, low key, and the child sweet and well behaved. So I told her it might work but I'd need to meet her man before signing anything.

Fine with that, she asked if we could sign a lease the following day and said she'd bring her boyfriend to meet me before we signed.

She arrived the next day with only her daughter though, no boyfriend, and gave some reason why he couldn't make it.

I didn't know what to do. I knew I should meet everybody who'd be living on my property...but after striving so long to find renters, I was relieved to have a solid little family. In this slim-pickin's market, with strenuous competition from other fretting landlords, it seemed unwise to stall even a day in getting the lease signed.

So, making an assumption that the man had to be alright since she presented so well, I signed a twelve-month lease with the woman. In that ailing economy, I believed I was saving myself future angst by securing tenants for a full year rather than six months.

LESSON : Don't make assumptions, especially about potential tenants you haven't met.

A day later, when they were moving in, I came out to greet them. And the moment I laid eyes on the boyfriend, who skulked in the driveway at the sight of me, I knew I'd blown it. I walked over to shake his hand, but his aura was so if-y I knew—and so did the woman, who looked on with concern—that if I'd met him earlier, I wouldn't have accepted them.

Clearly, the lady had stepped forth as the credible one, and...they were probably hiding something.

Oh, and they were.

Drugs.

And alcohol.

But the drugs were the main problem.

It turned out the guy wasn't "looking for work" or whatever she had told me, but was a stay-at-home ~~drug addict~~ dad.

Through this pair, I learned that in the State of Hawai'i, any single mother with a part-time job qualifies for welfare, additional funding for each child. This explained why they weren't married and why *she* had the part-time job. Meanwhile he, single man with no job, qualified for both welfare and unemployment. So he was always home—with the poor infant and the little girl—usually drinking with his posse of lay-about buddies.

These were also the ones to educate me that it's legal to drink and party all day in your own home, even outside in the yard, right up until 10 p.m.

That dude was a mess. Went out of his way just to disturb me—like placing big stones in the driveway where I parked, damaging my plants, sawing open the padlock on my storage closet. And in a matter of weeks, the little girl, who was becoming my friend, was instructed not to speak to me anymore. If her parents saw us chatting outside, she was abruptly summoned indoors. And soon she stopped even saying hello.

But I got stuck with those charmers *for a year*, and not just as renters, but as housemates.

However, it was through them, too, that I came up with raising the rent as a means of ousting sadsack tenants. Because, when renewing a lease, you can charge whatever you want, and no one can challenge it (unless there's rent control in your district). So in this case of negativity and distrust, that's what I had to do.

But those folks left an imprint on me. Literally. After they vacated, the dirty diaper smell from the giant trashcan remained, so I had to scrub it out. Filling the bin with soapy water, I stuck a long brush down there to reach the bottom. But all that water was incredibly heavy, and while pushing the bin across the yard to dump the water onto the grass, the open lid snapped up and banged my forehead so hard I flew through the air and onto my back, blood gushing from my head.

That scar is my souvenir of those happy times. *LESSON :* Tough experiences may leave scars.

Also, when cleaning inside the house after they left, I spied a tiny, pencilled message camouflaged onto the dark wood on the lower part of the little girl's bedroom door. It read, "I hate my mommy."

HUD

Everyone's heard of Housing and Urban Development (HUD), a federal subsidy providing people free rent for a year, two years, or longer. Recipients adore getting into the HUD program, that often has a long wait list. And these tenants are usually placable in order to keep their blessed benefits. But HUD landlords and their properties have to meet certain criteria, including committing to a full-year lease and providing well-backed reasons if they don't want to renew. So if your unit is idiosyncratic, makeshift, boot-legged, or lacking in some capacity—no door, meaning tenants have to climb in a window, or it's a yurt with an extension cord to your back patio—you won't qualify. Also, HUD reports to the IRS, so any year you house HUD renters, expect a 1099. Another consideration is that HUD recipients frequently aren't working, nor anxious to start since they have free rent. But again, it's a government contract, so you need a strong reason to get HUD tenants out.

But HUD has pluses. An unbounceable check arrives, without fail, on the first of each month; HUD recipients may be awesome tenants since they want to STAY; and aside from Uncle Sam's generosity, they also appreciate that you took them, where many landlords won't.

And if that's your leaning as well, state in your ad, "Sorry, unable to accept HUD," so a half-hour interview doesn't end with, "By the way, do you take HUD?"

For me, working tenants are preferable. But remember, I'm discriminatory. HUD might be just dandy for you. Some landlords swear by it.

As you've surely noticed, I lacked all natural proclivity for landlording. And after about six years, though the debt was slowly shrinking, I was still waiting for the learning curve to start *curving*. Instead, there was ever some new diabolical twist from those whose home was technically mine.

But through it all, I stayed in the game.

And then one day, I unearthed a piece of folded yellow paper from the bottom of a bureau drawer. I didn't even recall what it was…. Opening it, there they were, all the fears I'd listed, all the calamitous scenarios meant to evaporate after writing them down, all that dread I'd released to the universe that twilight moment on the beach. And right around now I was supposed to be laughing out loud, looking back at how foolish I'd been to doubt myself.

But that wasn't my reaction.

Far from it.

Because *every single fear* I'd listed had actually come to pass…and then some.

With my remaining $400,000 of debt still glaring from tattered spreadsheets—along with another fluke accident, broken bones, a surgery, and hardware in my leg—I decided to move out of my lovely House #1 and let tenants cover that mortgage too, while I spent more time with my dad on Long Island.

Tenants know how to time their dramas though, waiting until you're with your ancient father six thousand miles away to text that they're breaking the lease and moving out.

20

Trisha

Trisha Skinner gets a chapter of her own.

I had rented a room next door to my father's retirement community on Long Island in order to spend precious time with him, but on this occasion, was returning to Kaua'i to interview new tenants for my front unit. Having already advertised on Craigslist and done phone screenings, I would begin interviewing immediately upon arrival.

Forty-year-old Trisha, fresh from Georgia, had called me the day before my flight. Robust and eager, she provided the details of her household, that included her step-sister Becky (same age range and who'd be getting a job right away) and Pops, an elderly, disabled vet with all the benefits, for whom Trisha was the caregiver. The final housemate would be Hank, Trisha's husband of twelve years, currently driving across country in a car he'd be shipping to Kaua'i from the West Coast. Trisha explained that Hank, previously employed by Hewlett Packard, would also be finding immediate work on island.

Though a more astute landlady might've earmarked certain subtle indicators, I didn't initially perceive Trisha as problematic. Overly gung-ho perhaps, but she offered me $200 a month higher rent than I was asking (the subtle indicator I fell for), wanted to move in right away, and appeared to have her wits about her. "It's so hard to find a place," she pitched over the phone in her southern drawl. "The market is really, really tight and competitive. So since we need something right away, we're prepared to pay $200 a month extra, since we just got to the island. And since there are four of us, that's only $50 extra each."

"Deals" on Kaua'i have always been few and far between, so Trisha's offer wasn't off the wall. But since they hadn't seen the place, I suggested she might be putting the cart before the horse. But she claimed my Craigslist description matched their needs to a tee. And expecting competition for the unit, she even offered to pick me up at the airport to win first viewing when I touched down.

A lift from the airport is always welcome, plus my car was parked in the garage at the rental house, so I'd be heading there anyway. And having Trisha chauffeur me in exchange for being first applicant seemed a win-win, while the eight-minute ride with her might prove insightful.

As planned, Trisha and Becky—animated blondes, a tad flamboyant but otherwise plausible—met my plane. And once at the property, they *loved* everything about it and emphatically wanted it!

Like all newcomers, they were delirious to be on Kaua'i, and said the rent, even with $200 extra, was workable since they all had income or soon would. We chatted for over an hour at the property—me with my usual queries, and the ladies assuring me they were clean, hardworking, didn't drink, and would be taking care of Pops, who'd arrive within the week, with Hank close behind.

Having what could be a decent set of tenants (and mostly family) right there waiting and even paying extra, was hard to resist…. But I didn't just hand over the keys. To bide time, and since I was wasted from the red-eye, I said I'd think it over and we'd speak again on the 'morrow.

LESSON : Always "sleep on it" whenever there's even the slightest doubt regarding big or expensive decisions. (And not just in landlording.)

With rest and rumination, I decided that, even without the extra rent, these prospects were related, working, non-drinkers, and clean—the c-word a rare and weighty factor for me. There were no children, no animals, and only one vehicle. So, under the condition that I must meet both Pops and Hank upon their arrival, I signed them on for six months.

The gals jumped right in and in no time were cheerily cleaning and watering plants. Trisha could usually be found in the front yard in her bikini, and both babes, always at home, seemed blissed out just to keep house on a tropical island.

A week later, I got the intro to the not-so-sprightly Pops. This Southern boy was…definitely unusual, but alert, personable, and kind of a softie. Though virtually immobile, he had that attentiveness of many vets. And the arrangement, apparently, was that Pops would be home all the time and Trisha, his paid aide, would see to all his needs.

Since the ladies were bubbling over with friendliness and held nothing back, it was revealed that Becky had an autistic, twenty-year-old son back in Georgia, who was staying with his grandmother. And though it seemed odd to me a mother would venture so far from a needy child, both women assured me things were fully under control.

And the following week produced Hank—low key, sharp, credible enough, and close to what I'd expected. Now the household was complete.

But not long after Hank's arrival, I learned Becky was returning to Georgia because her son was having brain surgery. He'd had ongoing issues, I was informed, and things had escalated. I was apprised, too, that a new family member would replace Becky—a younger brother, Billy, who worked in construction, would be jetting in.

About twenty-one, Billy, who I didn't meet right away, easily landed a well-paying construction job and began commuting by bus to the North Shore. And when I eventually caught up with him in passing, he seemed on the up and up, though didn't resemble Trisha in the slightest.

It had now become evident that Pops' lifestyle was to station himself on the couch and drink beer all day. Trisha was satisfied to have others paying the bills while she kept house in skimpy outfits, or gadded about the island. Hank took a back seat, pointedly disassociating from any intrigue that may or may not surface. It was all somewhat…peculiar. "But they're family," I tried to override any disconnects. "It's gonna be okay. So far, so good." And Billy, though I rarely saw him, was pretty straight with me.

But with Becky gone, Hank detached, Pops drunk on the couch, Billy never around—Trisha, the supposed ringleader, wasn't panning out as quite the grounding force she'd billed herself as. In fact, out and about a lot now, she seemed to have some other agenda altogether—leaving Pops alone and loaded, and Hank off at his new job at the Home Depot (my alma mater).

Then one day Pops phoned me, "Trisha's in jay-al."

He breathlessly recounted how she'd punched him in the eye, broken his glasses, and caused him to fall over and bang his leg on the coffee table. Being attacked and injured, his only recourse had been to call the police. The cops had appeared in short order, arrested Trisha for "elder abuse," and carted her off. The transgression was clear-cut to them, since only Trisha and Pops were at home, and since she was the caretaker and he was injured, terrified, and shaken up.

So Trisha was in the slammer.

She'd also been served a restraining order stating that, after completing her sentence, she was no longer permitted anywhere close to Pops. She *or* Pops could live in the house, but not both. Tough bananas for two individuals who co-wrote the book on co-dependence. But since Pops was the one paying the rent, he was the one to stay. Yet Trisha single-handedly ran the household…so it didn't bode well.

No one, lastly me, had a clue what would transpire once the jailbird flew free.

Meanwhile, no one was caretaking Pops. His keeper was in the cooler for several more weeks and would thereafter have a restraining order. Billy had his construction work, and Hank was full-time at the Depot. So I went to the property for a heart-to-heart with poor Pops, bruised and radically off kilter.

Though thoroughly sad and lonely, Pops was mellow by nature, and appreciated (needed) my support and sympathy. Utterly disenchanted with Trisha now, he was willing to divulge a few tidbits she'd prefer withheld from the landlady. For starters, she was a meth addict. Next, Becky wasn't really her step-sister—Pops was surprised I referred to her as such—but Trisha's lesbian lover she'd met in prison in Georgia.

Following an update like that, it's not easy for a landlady to simply resume her errands and grab lunch. Knowing Trisha was a drug addict, a liar, a con artist, a criminal, a two-timer, in custody, and God knew what else, plus not allowed on the property…was a lot of junk food for thought.

Conflicts amongst tenants are, by osmosis, the landlord's problem too, hopefully minimally but sometimes overwhelmingly. Though tenants like to imply it's none of your beeswax (Pops being the exception), it's totally your beeswax when they're out of line, lying to you, or committing crimes.

So how long would Trish be in the pokey? No one knew. "Not long," it was surmised. And she was such an operator, not much could keep her down. Regardless, it seemed like the "Tale of Trisha Skinner" couldn't have a happy ending.

To get his take on it, I located Hank at the Depot. But as I prodded for info, he just continued re-stocking supplies in the plumbing aisle, notably blasé considering his wife was locked up for "elder abuse and battery." Granted, he was at work—captive, definitely off guard, and surely embarrassed and uneasy—but he remained deadpan in light of the breaking news that would've floored a normal spouse. I'd eventually learn this was standard operation for Hank, straight man in this charade of a couple. But no further intel was mined through that encounter.

During the jail interval, I spoke regularly with Pops, partly out of concern for the abused substance-abuser, and partly to keep up with developments. Grateful for company while mending his wounds, Pops was more than willing to bat his issues around with me. Billy was helping him a little now and Hank was there at night, but Pops was over a barrel because Trisha was still technically his caretaker, still on the payroll, yet he wanted nothing more to do with the loose cannon.

With beer, meth amphetamine, elder abuse, and prison all featuring in this drama, I now identified Billy—who maintained he was, indeed, Trisha's real brother—as the only sound household presence. But he, too, confirmed that she was a con artist, addict, and frequent law breaker.

Eventually, I got wind that Trisha was out of the pen. So I dropped by to get the headlines. Bikini-clad and ripped to the eyeballs, she herself opened the door. Billy and Hank were at work, while the felon was exactly where she shouldn't be, with Pops. (Though her options were few.) Pops, freaking on his couch, was throwing me looks of, "Oh my God! Oh my God!" But Trisha was even more uneasy because *the landlady was on the porch* discovering her defiance of the restraining order.

Needless to say, she wouldn't let me in. Plus her state didn't suggest reasoning, negotiating, or conversing anyway. I think that was the occasion where she called me "a greedy grubber." So I took my leave.

After a spell, I phoned Pops and told him to just call me if he needed to, but that there wasn't much I could do right now that wouldn't add fuel to this blaze.

And later that day, I learned from either Billy or Pops that Trisha, knowing she couldn't linger there, had only gone to the house to collect her belongings. And in record time, she'd already worked her charms to secure a new caretaking position with another elderly gentleman up the road, and had taken up residence there.

But my rental was in critical condition. Pops had no caretaker and needed one. I can't remember if the lease was up, or we all (minus Trisha) just agreed it should be, but Pops then decided to go back to the Mainland, and a week later flew the coop. (I drove him to the airport and sincerely wished him well.)

Billy then became my eyes and ears there. But with Pops gone, Trisha was back in a flash. And now Billy wanted no part of what had become way too unpleasant, so he too left the island.

Now, with Hank all but invisible, it was back to me and Trisha, face to face. Without Pops' money, or Becky's, or Billy's, Trisha couldn't possibly make the rent and still afford drugs, so I was just waiting for her to vacate. That's when she casually stated she wouldn't be leaving because she knew what she could legally get away with. "I'm gonna stay here for another month and live out my deposit. And I'm not payin' rent. And…y'know, it's just too bad…there's nothin' you can do. And Hank's here, too."

"Yeah, but I'm not gonna have any deposit when you go."

"That's okay," she said, "I'll leave the place clean."

With tenants, you never know what they will or won't do. Their word is rarely their strong suit. And this was *Trisha*! But all I could do was wait out the month and see how it shook out. So I didn't challenge her, try to reason with her, or see any need to discuss what she'd made up her mind to do. I just left her alone and crossed my fingers.

The good news was that Trisha kept her word this time. She rode out her deposit, left on the first of the next month, and the unit was truly clean.

LESSON : Finances aren't the only thing to run a landlord off track. Tenant drama, drugs, lies, and uncertainty can cause more grief than a bounced check.

P.S. I learned later that Trisha Skinner went on to become notorious on Kaua'i, treating more landlords to her schemes. And Hank stayed with her...until their reputations forced them off island.

This place has a way of doing that.

21

Harvey the House Husband

Although Harvey and family rented my residential home, not my rental property, I can't exclude him from this narrative. Because the lengths and calculations this specimen went to were no less than stunning.

I was twelve years into landlording. Blessed Rosie had gone to the Happy Hunting Grounds, my debt was shrinking, my massage business thriving, I had several books published, and my main focus was now on spending as much time as I possibly could with my father, almost ninety-five.

A few years earlier, I'd relocated to Long Island for two six-month winters and, thankfully, had been on hand when most needed. And though Dad was hardly in an enviable position now—bedridden and in skilled nursing—he was doing remarkably well. He was carefully attended by my step-mother and dutiful, ever present nurses. And having established which medical protocols he'd comply with and which he definitely would not, he no longer needed my holistic backing as he had when his health first went haywire.

So it was best I return to my own life and just visit whenever I could. But that meant traveling a lot, so rather than moving back into my House #1, I rented a one-bedroom *pied-à-terre* on Kaua'i, from which I could come and go more easily. And I got renters for the house.

It was mid August and I was advertising for new tenants. A Mainland guy living on O'ahu called, saying he and his family and dog were moving to Kaua'i to buy a house.

I told him the shortest duration I could offer was five months—probably not workable for them if they were house hunting—because I needed to be with my father for Christmas and his 95th birthday in January.

"Oh, no, no, we're in no hurry to find a house," said the guy. "And even when we do, we'll still have to close escrow and everything. Five or even six months would be great. We know it's going to take time to find the right house."

"Well, in my experience," I countered, "finding a suitable house can happen at any time. And when you find it, you have to jump. Then once you own it, you want to move in as soon as you can because mortgage payments start immediately."

"No, we're really in no rush. We want to take our time and figure out exactly where on the island we'll want to be."

"But I would need you to honor the duration of the lease, even if you bought a house before the lease was over. The lease absolutely needs to go to February 1st because I'll be away in December and January. And I need to be on island for the moving in and out of tenants."

"Oh, we're definitely not going to find a house fast," he insisted. "Even if we did, we'd still honor our lease with you."

I was hesitant. Though this family fit the bill for what I sought, their house hunting concerned me…. "I'm talking about this up front because it's serious for me. I'm going to Long Island for what might be my dad's last Christmas and his birthday. I need solid tenants in the house until February 1st."

We went on to chat about other criteria. The man, Harvey, claimed to be a day-trader, while his ~~breadwinner~~ helpful wife worked for Kaiser and would be at our local hospital, about ten minutes from the house. That I accepted dogs (outdoor, Harvey assured me) made him even more eager to nab this rental. So I said I'd think about it and we could speak again in a day or two.

But Harvey eagerly phoned back the next day, lobbying hard that his family would meet all my qualifications.

"The only way I could do this," I said finally, "would be if I wrote a clause into the lease that stated, 'Even if tenants purchase a home and it becomes habitable before February 1st, they agree to honor the full duration of this lease, regard-less.'"

"I assure you that would be NO problem," said he. "Whatever happens with our home buying, we can promise we'll still abide by the terms of the lease. And I'm not even worried about it because I know there's no way we'll be ready to move before February 1st. In fact, I'm glad we'll have five months."

You know where this is headed.... You probably also noticed I *didn't* follow the basic tenets of my own Sorry School for Tropical Landlords. Like meet all your occupants and dog before signing them on. Why didn't I? Because I was still *learning* the lessons back then. Thus, I overlooked the screaming clue, "I'm a day-trader and my wife works full time." The two ~~house husbands~~ stay-at-home dads I had the displeasure of renting to caused me more strife than any other tenants.

However, I can forgive myself for not meeting this family beforehand because Harvey and his wife wouldn't have flown over from O'ahu for an interview anyway. Plus, in person, they were relatively convincing, and I probably would've taken them. But the fact is, in faraway lands where about half your applicants are an airplane ride away, there will be repeated occasions where phone calls are your only means of "meeting" them.

To summarize Harvey's antics: First off, they rented my house fully furnished. So, having just dealt with the previous tenants storing all their earthly possessions inside this house, I asked where Harvey's own furniture would be put. To which he replied they'd be renting a storage unit until they bought their house.

Next, upon their arrival, the first thing I observed, aside from the two overtly *sad* children, was that the outdoor dog was always inside and barking incessantly.

Then, just a month into their Kaua'i life, Harvey left me a voice message, "You need to come and grab your bed, because our bed has arrived and we're sleeping on that now."

Insulted by the language—no one "grabs" a queen-sized bed, especially a single female with a small sedan, who has nowhere to put the thing—I called to say that my bed needed to stay in the house, as agreed to. To which Harvey retorted that it was roach-infested (my pristine gift bed from Scott) and he refused to sleep on it (though he just had for four weeks), and if I wouldn't grab it, he'd put it in the carport.

Then, ruffled when I didn't grab the bed, Harvey soon sent over a photo of a scorpion in one of my kitchen pots.

Since I'd never before seen a scorpion on my property, and only one on the whole island—in fact, I suspected his photo was of a plastic insect since Halloween was near—I just replied, "Well, I'm glad no one got stung, but this is the tropics."

LESSON : If tenants are taking pictures of "issues" at your property, there's likelihood they're collecting exhibits for the judge for when they soon default on the lease.

The next incident was when my gardener, who mowed both my properties twice each month, reported that Harvey had fired him. Harvey the House Husband told the gardener he was no longer needed, then borrowed a lawnmower from the next-door neighbors and mowed the lawn himself.

Containing my outrage, I went straight over to inform the free thinker that, per our lease, the gardener was part of the package and that he worked for me, not Harvey, and would continue. I added that if Harvey wasn't comfortable with the arrangement, he shouldn't have rented from me, because everything had been spelled out precisely in our first conversation and written in the lease.

Obviously, this stock trader had too much time on his hands, since the stock market closes at 10 a.m. Hawai'i Time.

But Harvey's next stunt seriously derailed me. The first week of November, he announced that they'd bought a house and were moving out December 1st.

I, of course, asserted that this was in violation of our signed agreement and, silently seething, did everything I could to convince him to honor the lease and wait until February 1st. Though he and his wife well knew my reason for needing them to stay, apparently their word was turd.

Now, knowing I'd be interviewing tenants at Christmas instead of visiting my dad, I suffered through thoughts of him bedridden, away from family, and alone on Christmas Day.

Meanwhile, displeased by my negative response to his lease breaking, Harvey began fabricating his next ruse. He now placed an ad on Craigslist stating that the house, where he was still living, was for rent and interested parties should "stop in this Saturday and Sunday afternoon to pick up an application." In other words, just show up without appointments. And he posted the address.

That weekend, indeed, eager renters came knocking. That's when Harvey phoned me, feigning outrage, and accused ME of posting the ad. How dare I invade his family's privacy like that?!

Yet only Harvey would've put that ad up; only he was devious enough to cook up such a ploy. So I phoned Craigslist to get to the bottom of it. They said they couldn't divulge who'd placed the ad but, if subpoenaed for a court case, *would* reveal its author. And that was all I really needed. And when I phoned Harvey to share that Craigslist would provide the ad's author if push came to shove, he dropped the accusation as if it never happened.

I'd warned this boorish lout before he moved in or signed the lease that he wouldn't get his security deposit back if he broke the lease. Now he just shrugged me off and they moved out December 1st.

Very mad and very sad, I knew that even if I quickly found new renters, I couldn't immediately leave the island without being sure all was running smoothly.

But Christmas season isn't a popular moving time. So, between infrequent interviews, I just performed sage smudgings to clear Harvey's residue from my beloved home.

And unrelated to the Harvey antics, but shortly after his family vacated, a massage shop I'd never heard of called to offer me a position. Being established in that business, I knew massage places don't reach out to therapists, but the other way around…so it was weird. I asked the woman on the phone how they got my name, and she said from the Internet, where, in fact, my presence was practically nonexistent. Still she continued persuading me to come in and meet them, touting all they would offer, like I could make my own hours and need only accept massage jobs on my side of the island. But this off-the-wall offer was…just odd, plus I already had all the work I could handle.

In massage, though, success has everything to do with saying yes all the time. So when they called a second time, I agreed to try to stop by.

And a week later, I marched up to their reception desk, gave my name, and asked if the boss was in. That's when the receptionist passed me a white envelope with my name on it.

"What's this?"

"It's for you. The boss isn't here right now, but she said to give you this."

Confused, I stood there momentarily, then figured it must be their application form, so unsealed the envelope and looked inside. Though I had no cause for suspicion, the dots weren't connecting…. So with one finger, I poked apart the folded letter inside to see what it was.

There, typewritten on troublingly official letterhead, I saw Harvey's name and my own.

And I needn't see more. I asked the receptionist for some tape, taped the envelope closed, placed it on her counter, and walked out.

Though that letter looked rather formal, I knew nothing about "being served." Frankly, I'd never heard of it. Not sure how I missed that whole reality, since everyone else seems well aware of it. But for the few individuals as naive as I, "being served" means being handed, in person, written notification that you are officially summoned to court. The document now in your hand includes all the details of the case, and has been ordered by the plaintiff of said law suit in which YOU are the defendant. Have a great day!

To make sure you don't refuse any white envelope being thrust at you—like maybe you guess what it is and want no part of it—the "server" is normally someone you've never met who's been hired to deliver it. That way, you unwittingly accept it, to discover what it is upon opening. And while shoving the envelope into your unsuspecting mitts, the server will usually state, "You've been served," then swiftly depart.

One more educational aspect of landlording to get your brain around. Trouble is, if you're "served"—as I guess I was on that occasion (though I retain doubt that it's legal to serve someone by duping them with a bogus job offer)— that letter announces the date and time of your court case. But if you don't open it or don't read past the first two lines, like I didn't, you're clueless about the scheduled event.

And you may miss it completely…like I did.

And to further my education, I next learned that as a no-show for a court date, you automatically lose your case. And the plaintiff, i.e. Harvey, automatically wins! Have a nice life! *LESSON :* Never be a no-show in a court case. You LOSE by default.

At least I did know by then that courts don't help winners retrieve monies won. That hefty challenge has to be orchestrated on one's own.

While missing Dad's final Christmas, that sadly it was, the last thing I wanted to do was hand back Harvey's security deposit. But he'd now won it by default. So, at a loss for options, I went to an attorney for the first time in my life.

Jay, my lawyer, was awesome. Even free, thanks to my freshly acquired senior status. And bizarrely, Jay himself had recently sublet my little *pied-à-terre* for a month, when I'd briefly slipped back to Long Island, so he, ironically, had first-hand experience with me as a landlady. Never guessing we'd soon be attorney and client, we'd had a smooth-as-silk rental experience. Plus I'd gotten to know and like him because we'd frequently spoken on the phone since he was tending my little cat.

Also, like Harvey, Jay had moved from O'ahu, and had also rented sight-unseen and without meeting me. So this case fit him like a glove.

Jay's professional advise was that, if I intended to keep the security deposit—based on the house being empty in December while I had to search for new renters, as well as other costs Harvey's early departure had caused me—I needed to show these losses in writing. More importantly, I'd need to show that Harvey owed me more than I owed him (the amount of the security deposit).

Great, great advice…though I didn't actually comprehend it until it was illustrated later, in real time.

LESSON : If a landlord claims, in writing, that *tenant owes landlord* more money than the total security deposit (that tenant wants back), then tenant probably won't sue for the deposit because landlord can then countersue for what tenant owes him/her—which is more than the security deposit.

In court cases, we also always hear about compensation for "pain and suffering." In reality though, judges aren't liberal with "hardship" fees. "Of course it was hard for you, that's why we're all here today. All court cases are misery for all concerned." If you're asking for money for pain and suffering, judges want to see psychiatrist bills and medications rendered for your suicidal tendencies. Saying it was "a big bummer" won't cut it.

So I compiled a list of expenses Harvey had taxed me, and made sure the total was about $500 more than his security deposit. It took creativity. Then I sent Harvey a copy.

Around that same time, someone stole all the grapefruits off the big tree I'd planted in the back yard of my rental property! Over a hundred ripe fruits that I had a buyer waiting for. And then, weeks later, when the smaller grapefruits grew to size, they, too, were snatched—both thefts occurring when no one was home at that property. And I and all my tenants there were plumb stumped as to who could've done it, and when....

I didn't even think of Harvey.

But in the final analysis, there was no one else in my orbit with anything close to that malice, cunning, vengeance, motive, or time on their hands. And property ownership is public record, thus accessible to anyone seeking the address of your property.

December rolled by. And though I initially had my fingers crossed that I'd rapidly get new tenants and get to Dad by Christmas, it wasn't happening.

Then one afternoon, I was at the house under the mango tree, where I'd just found two tiny, featherless, baby birds fallen from their nest. One was dead, but the other still alive. So I was carrying the tiny thing back to the house where I would try to feed it. And who should suddenly appear, standing right there in my back yard?

Harvey was no casual drop-by. And though we chatted unassumingly for a moment, it didn't take long for him to declare he had come for his security deposit.

"I don't owe you anything," I said. "You, verbally and in writing, agreed to very specific terms of a lease that you then totally reneged on, with no concern how it affected and inconvenienced me. I told you how important it was for me to be with my father on Christmas, and thanks to you not keeping your word, I'm not going to be there."

"You owe me that money and I'm here to get it."

"I sent you a letter showing that you owe me more money than you say I owe you."

"Well, then I'll take you back to court."

"Fine, and I'll countersue."

"I'm here to collect my money, and you need to give it to me." I then noticed his car was parked on the shoulder of my property with his wife at the wheel, watching hard.

"You're trespassing," I said.

"You owe me that money."

"You're trespassing and you need to leave."

"I'll leave when I have the money."

"You need to leave right now or I'll call the police."

"I'm not leaving until I get the money."

My cell phone was handy and I dialed 911, "Someone's trespassing on my property and he won't leave."

"Are you in a safe place?" asked the 911 operator.

"We're both outside. I've asked him to leave but he said he won't."

"You need to go inside," she said, "and I'll send over the police. But you need to go indoors right now."

I paused for a second. Harvey stood his ground, and then his wife stepped out of the car and approached us like a prize fighter starting round one.

"Are you inside now?" asked the operator.

"No…."

"Go in now. That's what you have to do. The police are on their way."

So I went inside and left the couple fuming in the yard.

To avoid confronting the cops, Harvey and his wife angrily returned to their car and zoomed off.

Do you think that was the end of it? Do you think people like that take defeat in stride and get on with their cheery lives?

LESSON : Careful who you offend; some people stop at nothing.

Harvey waited several years, but kept his grudge.

P.S. And the baby bird survived, grew feathers, and a week later, *flew* back up into the mango tree.

22

Handling Legalities

Have I scared you back to lottery tickets yet?

If you still want to be a landlord, despite the last twenty-one chapters, first and foremost, trot down to your county or state office and obtain a copy of the Landlord/Tenant Guide. In Hawai'i, the booklet's about forty-five pages. This thing could be daunting if you had to study it for an exam, but for landlords, it's a friend, with all your rights spelled out. And you'll probably even find some surprises—for example, that some rules may lean in tenants' favor. But it's imperative that landlords know, honor, and live by the laws. As I've said, legal disputes (usually, but not always) boil down to written *law*. Knowing that will save you hot air, quandary, and discord.

With the passing years, I found myself more and more nonchalant in saying, "I go by the book. I have to go by the book."

How do you deal with rule breaking from your tenants? Well, it's a one-two-three, then an a-b-c-d, punch:

1. After your first awareness of an infringement, you have a conversation.

2. If things persist, you have a second, stronger conversation, possibly with a warning.

3. If nothing improves, tenants are given a letter and a time frame. The letter states a) what they're doing wrong, b) that you have verbally addressed it with them twice already, c) that they've implied they understood and agreed to comply, and d) that you still find the problem ongoing, so they now have two weeks to remedy the situation. You give them a little longer than you wish to, but not long enough to shrug it off.

All serious rifts must be dealt with in writing, clearly stating what you're asking of the tenants and the precise time period in which they're required to correct the problem. Maybe someone else has moved in, maybe they're making noise late at night, or maybe it's something mysterious you're confused about—like neighbors reporting a weird smell at 2 a.m., suggesting your dodgy lodgers are cookin' meth.

No matter the subject at hand, keep it polite and conversations brief. You're not coming on as a prosecutor, you're just explaining, "My job is to take care of the property, and the neighbors complained." Or, "It says in our lease that you're allotted two parking spaces, and you're taking three. Parking a third vehicle is not in compliance with the lease." Just state the issue, and if nothing changes, go back and address it again.

If they're dismissive or ornery when you approach them, and not doing anything about it, your letter will get the ball rolling.

But with nothing in writing, tenants may bamboozle the judge, "She never came over," or, "She spoke to Kiki, not to me. No one ever talked to me."

And if you merely contest that in court, "I specifically told them three times that they had to be quiet after 10 p.m.," all that will happen is the more-fetching-than-you tenant will step to the witness stand and say, "Your Honor, she never told me that." And that part of the claim gets dismissed as "he said/she said," while both parties are asked for something more concrete.

LESSON : In your warnings and in any letter, specify that, "It is expected that this message will be communicated to every member of the household." Name each one. Also state that the issue was previously addressed verbally on said occasions and that they must let you know, in writing, when they've complied.

With your letter in hand, the judge will sit there and study it. "Did you receive this letter?" s/he will ask the tenant.

"Yes."

"Did you respond to this letter?"

The tenant can't say, "Well, I don't agree with anything in it," because the judge will only ask again if the tenant responded in writing, and if so, where is that response?

Aside from seasoned anglers, tenants rarely take the time to reply in writing. So, fortunately, most of the documentation will be yours, not theirs.

In a court case, your job is to *show* (Exhibit A) what happened. For example, you sent this letter. Then two weeks later, you sent another letter (Exhibit B) saying, "I sent you a letter giving you two weeks to move the car and you didn't move it." The paper trail is mandatory because it's the only proof you'll ever have that any of this merriment took place. And too much is better than too little.

Believe me, you'll never *feel like* writing letters to tenants. But you could, indeed, end up in court one day. I was there three times in one year, the only court cases of my entire life. So be prepared to write letters now and then. You can even write in longhand, just print neatly. Make it a business letter, date it, make photocopies, and keep one in your files. With everything in writing, there's a concise statement, dates, and proof the letters were delivered.

LESSON: Anything without proof holds no weight with a judge.

If writing isn't your strong suit, just summarize your bullet points in a rough draft. "I'm writing: because a), b), and c). And what is expected of you is: a) or b)." Then flesh out the details in a second draft. Keep it courteous, to the point, easy to understand—never harsh, impatient, or condescending. Avoiding negative innuendo, just stay semi-cordial, "Per our lease agreement, no one may reside in the home except those on the lease. And I notice that you have your friend Joey living there now. This is not acceptable." I always signed off with a friendly tone, "I hope you're having a nice summer." Not "hugs and kisses," but at least, "With Aloha," or "Sincerely."

Proofread your letter *several times* before delivering. You'd be amazed how a minor omission or oversight can tangle you up in court. And tenants can be devious and clever, intentionally tripping you up over minutia. Don't underestimate their shrewdness or courtroom finesse. They may even be advised by an uncle who's a cop or a granny who's a judge. So dot your i's, cross your t's.

But DON'T refer them to page 16 of the Landlord/ Tenant Guide Book, article 2-C, section VIII. That's interpreted as annoying and provocative. "We have to somehow dig up that obscure rulebook and read the thing? Give me a break." Quote the booklet if you want or need to— it's helpful to refer to something official if you're hitting a wall with tenants—but legalese comes across as overbearing. It's softer to say, "Please refer to your lease, page 2, section 8, where you'll see the subject addressed," or "You'll see on your lease where it states so-and-so."

Another reason not to direct them to the rulebook is because they'll then have a copy of it—and this happened to me—to go through with a fine-toothed comb for something to pin on *you*. Maybe, like me, your back kitchen isn't fully up to code. There might even be some noncompliance you're unaware of.

Then drop the letter off at their unit. And minimize its gravity by saying, "This is just to document what we talked about when I came by last week." When delivering written correspondences, you can hand it to them or mail it. "Certified" isn't a bad idea, particularly if you'd prefer not to see or talk to them—but that can be perceived as heavy-handed, making them hostile or heavy-handed in return. I usually just taped it to the front door and took a picture of it there.

I'm *not* litigious. Most people aren't. It's a wretched pastime. But when I did end up in court three times in a row, Jay said, "Well, the good thing about all this is that you're learning how courts work."

"I don't want to know how courts work," I reached for another tissue, partly because both my father and sister had died right in the middle of my worst case.

"It's really good to know," Jay asserted. "You never know when you might be in a court case, and it's important to understand the process."

He was so right.

23

Gangsta Tips

Release any "perfect tenant" notions in ~~year~~ month one of this profession. In our world, there are just too many opportunities for misunderstanding, misinterpretation, monkey biz, deceit, and funky weirdness. Because a person's need for shelter and their ability to pay for it don't always go hand-in-hand, even minor kerfuffles between landlords and tenants often involve more than meets the eye. Late payment of rent, for instance, can mean money issues, family issues, career issues…and always emotion. Even when everyone's acting like it's a normal Tuesday. (Think Hank.) Maybe the tenants are getting divorced, someone got fired, someone's having an affair, someone lied, someone's sick, or someone's in the slammer.

But you won't be in the loop, so you're stuck taking tenants at their word. Still, when something's in the air, something's in the air…and you may duly wonder, "What's going on over there?"

Oh, you'll find out.

But truth be told, doing your absolute best will get you through. If you've authentically listened, and been fair to them, you should be able to sleep at night.

On the other hand, there *will* be occasions when even your best won't alleviate the problem, and you can't sleep at night. But with time, we learn the ins and outs and work-arounds. Sometimes we even invent solutions.

Here are a couple of strategies I employed in my later landlord days.

Getting Advice and Estimates

The first one is simply an approach to construction projects and home-building professionals, and isn't at all uncommon, but worth spotlighting.

Let's say you want to build a porch or redo your bathroom…anything from building a fence, to upgrading your kitchen, to adding an apartment over your garage. If construction isn't your forte, where do you begin? How do you explore all the options, costs, and hidden ramifications? Who do you ask, how do you budget the project, what supplies will you need and what tools, who should you hire, what kind of a timeline should you expect? Not to mention all the tangents, like what's the sequencing of tasks, can it be done in stages, how long might it take, where do you buy materials, can you get discounts or installments on payments, and are there portions of the project you could do yourself?

Before you start, when you're considering who to hire, interested professionals that you contact will stop by to assess the job and possibly bid on it. And during obtaining estimates is your golden opportunity to gather insight, opinions, and options pertaining to your project. This is the one occasion when the exact people you need to consult with are willing, even eager, to give you FREE advice. At this moment only, they're off the clock and, if they want the job, need to win you. So discussing how they'll perform the work is how they prove they're knowledgeable, experienced, legit, and just the person you need. And they fully understand that giving an estimate doesn't guarantee getting the job. So don't feel you're usurping their time; you have every right to understand in detail what will take place and what it will cost. Scrutinizing various approaches to a project is how you map your path forward, and you're actually foolish if you don't ask a lot of questions. Plus these estimates are *a free service,* hence your best shot at gleaning all the expert advice you can. (Without, of course, seeming like a complete....) *LESSON :* In the construction trade, giving an estimate, diagnosing the issue, and discussing the game plan with the homeowner are prerequisites for getting a job.

In a nutshell, when offering a gig, *you* have the power. But only beforehand will these guys indulge your visions and queries, maybe even wax creative with you. Once hired, you'll pay by the hour for brainstorming.

And since each pro has a unique approach, it pays to invite several over for estimates. Confabulating with each, you can then take a little from this guy, a little from that one, and piece together a plan. One might emphasize a nice paint job to complete the work, where another might say, "Oh, I wouldn't paint it, I'd stain it." One might say, "Drywall's my thing, I can drywall with my eyes closed, it'll only take a day. And I have some extra drywall in my garage left over from another job that I'll give you for half price." While another might say, "I'm a carpenter/builder—you'll need to hire someone else for the drywall." One might say, "I charge a lot, but you're going to get the best work there is. I'm da man."

Another might say, "Oh no, no, honey, your concept is seriously flawed, and here's why." Some guys are super creative and thrive on that element of construction, others are all about saving you money. They're all different! But *combining* their breadth of ideas, you can quilt together an outline way more viable than the piecemeal premise you started with.

But don't abuse this—it's just an interview for a job, they're not consultants. Couch your questions informally, like, "Well, one of the things we want to do here is change the flooring. I'm thinking of tiling. Do you have experience with that?"

He may answer, "Have you considered laminate flooring?"

"Well, what are the advantages of that?"

And his answer can lead to your next question, "Oh, that's an idea. How would that be preferable to tiling?" or "Have you done that a lot? What's the reason you recommend that?" Based on this exchange, you may change your whole vision and do your bathroom per his suggestion, because he's given you new info. And this may be the guy for the job.

Or you might decide, "Stuart's good at framing, Paul's good at painting—I'll hire them both." Or you could conclude that building this outdoor bathroom is more convoluted and expensive than you thought, and you better save more money and do it next year. Or never.

Most tradesmen will recommend either a) what's cheapest, and/or b) what's easiest to install, and/or c) what they have the most experience with, and/or d) "Whatever you want, dear. I'm here to build what you want." Obviously, a carpenter will recommend wood where possible. But a lot depends on how you pitch to them. One might veer way off, suggesting marble from the mines of Zimbabwe because he smells an upscale job, naive homeowner, or both.

And there can be gaming going on, and vibing both ways…you're reading each other. So it's important to genuinely click on some level. But straight-shooting, hard-working guys are out there. *LESSON :* Have an interview long enough to get a solid take on the person.

If he's flirting with you—trying to charm you and he might—if he's seriously late and doesn't alert you by text, if he changes the appointment time at the last minute, if he's rushed and has too much going on elsewhere, has his baby in the truck, or drives a sedan instead of a truck….beware. The list goes on: drinking a beer, lives too far away, stands you up, says he won't be available 'til next month, charges an arm and a leg….

It's also worth asking a property manager or realtor for a few referrals.

But without seeming like you're just getting all the free advice you can, get all the free advice you can! Some of these guys are storehouses of knowledge. And this is the time they'll "go there," chat about possibilities (a woman's dream), and you won't be billed. You can be honest, too. "I'm just exploring options right now. And getting estimates to find out how much it all will cost." (Though I wouldn't say, "Oh, I'm just having a bunch of guys come and give me ideas, then I'm gonna tackle it on my own.")

Another huge reason for interviewing several professionals is to get a detailed breakdown of expenses. Including costs of materials (brace yourself). Some workers pride themselves in giving a good deal, that's how they keep the jobs coming in, where others bill themselves as "the best" and make their money by charging top dollar. The majority are somewhere in the middle, aiming to deliver what was agreed to while not exceeding their estimate by too much. And it's also legit to feel them out and try negotiating or asking if they're flexible. They may be floating a high price to see if it lands. But most journeymen know what they need to charge to make it worth their time, and will tell you straight.

When my negotiating attempts are met with firm resistance, I just say, "Well, I've learned it never hurts to ask." And I'm then glad to know where the guy stands. But he's learning, too, that you're not rolling in dough, and cost matters to you.

But don't be a chiseler, or expect to pay yesterday's wages for today's labor. Everyone knows what we're doin' here is *expensive*. That's why God made the Home Depot, so you can attempt to do it, or some of it, yourself. But these guys, (except the wild boys who ride booms then move on), are largely family men who work really hard and take pride in what they construct. And they need to earn enough to feel good about working hard. So pay them fairly and help a good man make a living.

They Stay but Don't Pay

Another pro-landlord move I came up with—proud of this one—was what to do when a lease is ending and you're not renewing it for whatever reason, but your tenants elect to stay anyway. And not pay you anymore.

Such scenarios come by surprise. Aside from Trisha, tenants don't announce in advance, "By the way, we're not moving out on the first, we're just gonna stay but not pay anymore." They just…casually…don't leave, and you… slowly…figure it out. Then the weeks trickle by and you pay the mortgage.

But since these rough riders are usually more familiar with the laws than newbie landlords, just consider them *teachers*. The worst part, though, is that you *don't really know* what they're going to do, or when….

"We TOLD YOU we're leaving at the end of the month," they may repeat, like you're a moron. But how can you believe someone who at this very moment is working you? *Will* they leave when the deposit's used up? Or will you end up in court, need the marshal to eject them, and spend several months without income while they kick back in the shade of your plumeria tree? Meanwhile, are they respecting your property or trashing it? And are they crafting hostile scenarios to throw at a judge?

But, though aware they're being naughty, sitting tenants don't see this as "not paying the rent and staying for free." They pretend there's nothing wrong here, "Lady, you've got a month's rent on deposit. Why are you so upset? You ALREADY GOT the rent money." And fortunately for you, their chief aim is usually to just not pay, rather than to destroy your property or wish you ill.

For landlords, though, the not knowing is exasperating. And it doesn't dissipate until they finally drive away with whatever they don't leave for you to sort through. (Plus you'll probably learn that pills, drugs, or alcohol governed these tenants' every waking hour, explaining their hair-trigger temperaments.)

Problem is, as covered in earlier pages, when they do finally vacate, with no deposit money coming back to them, they have little incentive to clean the unit or remove their junk.

But people who stay without paying have probably done it before. So even if they appear open to discussion, they're just spinning your wheels—their minds are made up and they know the laws work in their favor. So, in these pickles, there's really no point in trying to "work things out" with them. After one all-out attempt to clarify the situation, I don't recommend reaching out again *at all*. Don't contend with them or even follow up, because there's *nothing* you can accomplish at this juncture. And definitely don't let them see you ruffled or showing anger.

Here's the deal, *they* may lose their cool, *you* may not. Because if you do, everything can backfire. Get them irked, and there are even more rules they can break—on *your* property, in *your* house. They can wreak havoc, even to your good name. Legally, they can even dig in until you ultimately have to "serve" them and have the marshal dump them on the street.

Let *them* do the guessing instead, about what *you* might do. When you go quiet, it baffles them—you're not the irate landlady you're supposed to be. "Why has she gone silent? Is she consulting an attorney? Hiring a hit man? She DOES have a key to this place...."

Just go directly into legal mode (once you figure out what "legal mode" entails here), and put it all in writing so you've got your paper trail. After questioning them—either in person, or by phone if they're unruly or unpredictable— and hearing their intentions, write up something to the effect of, "If the rent isn't paid by such-and-such a date, I will have to take legal measures. But I urge you to comply with the lease instead, to avoid undue duress." (Your letter should boldly state that, per the lease, the security deposit may never be used as rent.)

But here's the fun ploy to make sure they, at least, do vacate once that security deposit is burned through: We obviously can't move new tenants in while those guys still occupy the unit, so they're banking on this grace period for the next full month…. However—and fully honoring the law—*if no one else holds a valid lease,* the owner always has the right to live at the property. And these tenants' lease expired on the first of the month.

So, just in case these lounge lizards were thinking of overstaying their unwelcome beyond this coming month, I would nonchalantly tell them that I myself will be moving in on the first of next month. And this slaps a real bookend on their holiday. They look at each other. "Y'know, she sounded serious…."

In truth, there's no way I'm gonna move in if the tenants are still in there. (Just imagine!) *But they think I'm going to.* And it's my legal right.

So now they're fearing that, come the first, I'll turn the front door key, enter, plant my toothbrush in their bathroom and settle onto their couch. And since no one in the world wants to share living quarters with their landlord, the trick is to have them totally believing you have no Plan B.

"But…are you going to put us on the street?" they may cringe.

"I don't really know where you will be going, but I *have to* move in on that date because I'm scheduled to. And my two brothers are coming over from the Mainland to live with me." (Whether you actually have two brothers is your secret.)

"Will she really move in if we're still here?" they wonder. So they say to you, "Well, we...we...we have nowhere to go...."

"Well, then...then...then we'll just all live together," you act like you really like them and it might be fun. And enjoy the blank looks on their faces as they visualize all of you in the kitchen at breakfast. I don't get into who'll be flipping the flapjacks and who'll do the laundry—they can decide those delegations amongst themselves—but you can be as sure as anything that the last thing a sitting tenant wants is their landlady watching *Survivor* in their La-Z-Boy.

But you just lightly repeat, like the chorus of a camping song, "Yeah...we'll just live together then."

The kumbaya thing about this, which I'm proud to have enacted at least three times, is that nowhere in the Landlord/Tenant Guide book does it state a landlord can't move in with illegal occupants (too bizarre to be addressed). The handbook only says that if there's no longer a valid lease, tenants *can stay there* until formally evicted. It doesn't say landlord can't join the party. So no judge can fry you for it.

Alternatively, you could change the locks and/or turn off the water and electricity to get leverage, but that's *majorly* provocative and begs for dire recourse. And judges despise stunts like that.

So just tell 'em you're moving in and watch 'em squirm *LESSON :* If no one is holding a valid lease, no one can deny that a) the landlord has the right to now live there, and b) the landlord has a key.

The beauty of this is that it works! A) Because the tenants know they're wrong and they're playing you. B) They've been thrown a curve. This has never happened before and their heads are whirling as to whether you can or will follow through. C) This can't possibly be legal, but… hm, it's not exactly illegal. And D) they have no way of determining whether you're bluffing, because you're the landlord, the grown-up around here. Landlords aren't pranksters, they're practically law enforcement.

But the greatest part of this is…*they leave.* They may wait until the last day, but they actually throw in the towel.

And if you never really made them mad or irked them, and you didn't, they may leave your place intact.

Taking the Edge Off

I never tried the following ruse, and it may have fallout I'm unaware of, but were I ever to be a landlady again, I might consider it.

I once got to chatting with a woman doing outdoor maintenance at a rental property near where I take walks. And she confided that, though she told tenants she was the property manager, she was actually the owner.

By pretending someone else owned the place, and that she was just the worker bee, this woman felt she saved herself a lot of angst, possible blame, and ill feeling. Anything tenants approached her with, she would deflect responsibility or confrontation, and just say, "Well, I'll communicate that to the owner, and let you know how HE responds."

There's not much more I can say about it, since I never went that route myself. But think it over…and perhaps give it a try? I mean, if you have more than one unit, obviously you have to be consistent in what you tell tenants. The "coconut wireless" (word of mouth) is fast and furious on tropical islands. And if you live on the same property, where your life is transparent to tenants, I certainly wouldn't advise it. And don't forget that property ownership is public record, so people can find you out. But on the superficial level, this approach seems somewhat protective.

I just sense that lying could eventually backfire.

24

A Few Do's and Don't's

What You Don't Want :

Too many people, too many kids, dogs in cages, dogs as guard dogs, people without jobs, people who want to grow food, too many generations, people who want to store stuff (boats, horses), people with too many vehicles, auto mechanics, lute players (or any musicians who practice at home), people who want very short-term (base camp), moon dancers, singers, smokers/drinkers/druggies, people with medical marijuana cards (pot smoking can be smelled three houses away), HUD/welfare recipients, only had their job a month, looking for a job, "works from home" (or pretends to), been sober three weeks, house husband, day-trader, new relationship, your own relative or good friend, "desperately" searching for somewhere to live, bottom feeders, wants a puppy soon, faith healers, situation too weird or unusual (gay lovers pretending to be siblings), bratty kids, bad credit (might be okay, depends...), seriously ill, getting seriously old, has support animal, wants to run a business out of the property (like a daycare center), too many grandchildren (that they care for at the house), run-down cars, remodels cars as a profession or hobby, morbidly obese (sue me, it's an illness), depressed, "social drinkers," people who look funky, vague entrepreneurs, wanna-be influencers, someone else is paying their rent ("Mom is helping out the first six months"), has latch-key kids, suspicious of you or "been tricked too many times," hates the world, won't answer your questions (hiding something) or accusatory about your questions, has pregnant animals.

Keep your desperation meter calibrated, both your own desperation and that of potential renters.

What You Do Want:

Non-smokers/non-drinkers/non-druggies, all adults have full-time jobs, ambitious, healthy, look well and have family routines, people proffering credible reasons why and when they have to move, church-goers (sue me, they're better than drinkers), sober for many years, love their kids, kids are involved in activities, cars are decent, possible close family in general region, people who've been married a long time, just one or two kids, pets who've been in the family a long time, health freaks, people who mention being anal or clean, nurses, postal workers, government workers, people with "regular" jobs, people who are or have been property owners, people saving up to buy their own home, siblings (sometimes), athletic people, full-time teachers, people who go to bed early, workaholics, people who work in the cleaning business, people who love the place, people whose job is nearby, geeks and nerds (boring is good), bomb designers, people with high-paying jobs, people who tell you straight what their plan is ("We're here 'til September, then moving to O'ahu." "I'm retiring in eighteen months and moving in with my daughter").

You must:
• Understand where you have power and where you do not.

• Cover every single detail before signing the lease.

• Understand that the lease signing is the last time you'll have their full attention. After that, you're "bothering them," practically trespassing.

• Provide the gardener, but they pay that fee (to you monthly with their rent).

• Stop by periodically to do some weeding or whatever, so they never know when you'll show up.

• Drive by at night, especially when you have new tenants, to make sure everything's as it should be, parking guidelines adhered to, no strange activity.

• Know the surrounding neighbors and cultivate good relations with them. Have some of their phone numbers. And let tenants believe you're tight with them.

• Let tenants believe you have other pals right up the road, that's why you may drive by on occasion.

• Never divulge your bank account number.

• Use a P.O. box and phone number for all your contact info. Don't divulge your residential address.

• Make the late fee no less than $50 and its effective day early in the month—like due after twelve noon on the 3rd of the month—incentivizing them to pay rent on time. If the late fee's only $20, as of the 7th of the month, you'll always be receiving late checks, possibly well after the 7th.

• If at all possible, keep a (locked) work area, shed, or closet somewhere on the property, so you have tools handy when you're working there. This also establishes your presence.

• Whenever possible, do repairs to the house whilst you have tenants. That way, you don't lose rent money when painting something minimal or mending a roof. Tenants rarely mind, as long as you're considerate, give them advance notice, and work is done quickly, because they understand upkeep and they benefit from improvements.

• Immediately fix anything that breaks, because a) you should, b) then you don't have to do it when the unit is empty, and c) letting repairs accumulate will cost you a bundle when tackled all at once.

• Conduct regular inspections. For any lease over six months, tenants should expect inspections. (But give forty-eight hours' notice.)

• Make it known that you are allowed to be outside on the property at any time and without notice, and inside with twenty-four hours' notice.

• Never enter an occupied unit without twenty-four hours' notice.

• Never make noise on the property (you or your workers) without alerting tenants in advance that noise will be occurring.

• Never block tenants' entrances.

• Never park in tenants' spaces.

• Never bring your friends or family over for more than a few minutes or for a very specific reason—like your brother's a roofer and you have to check the roof with him.

• Never look in their windows, even if you think they're not home, except in emergencies. ("The neighbor said she saw you looking in our windows when we weren't home!!")

• Be friendly, but don't accost them with information, questions, or conversation when they're arriving or leaving the home. They're busy with their lives and this isn't fair to them. When you're gardening or working at the property, leave them alone unless they initiate something with you.

• Never go to their work place to find them—in order to address an issue, or because you've been unable to reach them, or for any other reason—unless it's truly your last-ditch means of connecting with them in person, in which case explain that and even put it in writing. ("Your Honor, she stalked me at my work place!")

• Don't do anything that could be misconstrued as rude, imposing, illegal, or intimidating. You have to be milder, more patient, and more courteous than normally befits all situations, because some tenants are looking for things to pin on you. Beneath your cool demeanor though, they should sense that you're no cream-puff.

• Never try to be their friend or consider them a buddy. Even if you really like them or think they like you, or even if they've lived on your property for years, any camaraderie you establish can vanish over the smallest skirmish. After they move out, you'll likely see they were only friendly because you had their money on deposit and they wanted a follow-up reference from you. So don't get chatty with the Mrs. on the porch some sunny afternoon. Next thing you know, you've divulged some personal vulnerability (your siblings hate you or you loathe being a landlord) or some deep confidence (like the time you were abducted by the Gentle Lizard People). These reveals will not be used in your favor.

• Take nearly the full two weeks to return their deposit (legal in Hawai'i), so you have time to spot any and all loss or damage. It can take a while to notice things damaged or even missing. *LESSON :* Advise tenants in advance *and write it in the lease,* that they'll receive their deposit, or balance due, within two weeks after they vacate. But never pay them late or make them wait until the 14th day.

• Never be desperate. Considering the inconvenience to your life and cost to your nerves of housing lousy lodgers, an occasional month of lost income is better than six months of aggravation.

LESSON : In order to hold out for responsible renters, keep enough money available to cover the weeks, or even months, when a unit may sit empty.

• Hire a legitimate inspector. Overlooking critical issues, Quack Frank colored everything for the duration of my rental property ownership. Though it seemed sensible at the time, letting my realtor recommend somebody was stooopid. Any "inspector" getting his jobs through a realtor obviously won't be sabotaging potential sales.

On the other hand, had a real inspector assessed all that house needed, I wouldn't have purchased it, may not have ended up financially stable, and you wouldn't be reading this book. So, as we all know, 'mistakes' can be fate-shifters, even divine guidance.

• During a renovation, lay out basic expectations for your workforce, stating things like, "We work clean on this job-site. You are responsible for your area. Don't leave a mess for me or for the next guy."

Most construction workers will look at you askance, "Construction's a messy thing, lady, everybody knows that." (And aside from Johnny, I never experienced exceptions to that mindset.) But at least buy some drop cloths, use them yourself, and have extras on hand. Also, insist drop cloths are shaken out over the trash bin. (Workers *adore* shaking paint scrapings and even old nails right onto the lawn.)

LESSON : Have on hand: a ladder, step-ladder, rags, old towels, newspapers, buckets, soap, sponges, toilet paper, and basic tools like a screwdriver, hammer, tape measure, exacto knife, level, painters' tape, a Sharpie, and solvents like Ajax, Goo Gone, and WD40.

LESSON : And although workers have their own tools, keep your own handy, in case someone forgets or loses theirs. And have extra supplies at the ready, like a roll of paper floor covering, sandpaper, nails and screws, paper towels, and a few cheapo paintbrushes.

LESSON : On day one, write your name, in paint or indelible ink, on all your own tools and equipment. And don't leave them lying around, especially in the presence of unfamiliar workers. It's no secret that tools vanish on construction sites. They either get misplaced in the pandemonium or unlabeled ones may actually get snatched.

• For sizable construction projects, having a truck is highly recommended and will also serve you afterwards. I wasn't about to ditch my brand new Prius (now twenty-four years old and still running like a dream), and didn't want two vehicles. But I didn't foresee how much hauling there'd be, how many trips to the dump, nor how many

Depot and lumber store runs ferrying stuff too big or too messy for my sedan. Even renting a truck, maybe one day a week, could spare you depending on workers, paid by the hour, to transport materials all the time.

• Have access to additional funding (kindly relations or jewelry to pawn), should things get out of hand. My final mistake was not having back-up resources. Things did get out of hand and I needed way more money than I had access to.

On the other hand, lean finances keep you careful. Spending is by far the easiest part of a construction project. Every single purchase has higher-end options—from who you hire, to upgraded fixtures, to cabinet knobs, to quality of paint, to bells, whistles, and flourishes.

Part V

The Home Stretch

≡ *25* ≡

Selling It

Despite the Promethean pleasure of restoring an old place and cultivating exquisite plants; despite the satisfaction of owning a piece of Paradise or "a slice of heaven," as property is known in da islands; despite the acquisition of new skills in construction, renovation, how to manage workers, how to use tools…landlording is, was, and always will be a money-making proposition. Keep that in the forefront of your mind, should you find yourself waffling about whether to sell. Don't let exasperation and impatience cloud your goal or sap your impetus. Barring extenuating circumstances, where you absolutely must sell—in which case, thank God you *have* something to sell—you need to be certain that:

- …you don't blow the whole scheme by selling too early. All that toil has to pay off!

- …that selling is really what you want now, that you won't regret it, and that you're clear about your next life calling.
- …that economically, this is an opportune moment in the housing market.

Selling in a down market can irreparably ding your hard-fought retirement platform, when another couple of years could mean $200,000 to $300,000 more toward geriatric bliss. So crunch your numbers HARD; selling *must pay off.* That's the sole purpose of this undertaking you've devoted a sizable chunk of your life to.

As you know, my aim was to pay off the house as fast as I could, then hold onto it free of mortgage payments, at which time I'd have income from both my units when I was old and grey. The property value would increase, and then around eighty, I'd have (my idea of) financial security, and could either continue collecting rent or sell.

But in the first few years, it became poignantly clear I'd never be at one with this walk of life. Because, no matter how sweetly or consciously you've sculpted your reality, the lives of tenants, particularly the wacky or misguided, affect your own. It's not easy to sail serenely along while repeatedly rubbing elbows with troubled souls.

Another stumbling block was the element of surprise— that anything can happen any time and how that thwarts your plans and inserts U-turns into your day.

Toward the end of my landlord tenure, when I was also still renting out my own residence, there was one Christmas season (before the Harvey year) when I begged all three sets of tenants, "I'm going to be with my very old father, who I rarely get time with and who doesn't even have a phone, so visiting him is the only way I can even talk with him. *Please, please,* do whatever you can to NOT call me over the next two weeks. If there's anything that can wait until I get back, please just give me those extra days."

Never a good idea to a) divulge personal data, b) expose your vulnerability, and c) ask of tenants something that you might ask of friends. But they all assured me, "Oh sure, of course! Don't worry! Yeah, yeah, go be with your dad. We'll be fine!"

Yet all three sets managed to call me on that trip, two suddenly vacating for fluke reasons, and one with a refrigerator crisis. And believe me, getting a phone call (at 9 p.m. local time) about a broken refrigerator when you're sitting beside your ninety-two-year-old, bedridden dad 6000 miles away, having a father-daughter heart-to-heart, is so crushing I still tear up at the memory. "I'm sorry, Dad, I really have to take this call." Then I returned to his room to see he'd fallen asleep for the night and we'd never finish that talk.

For me, ultimately, the recurring negatives of land-lording outweighed the promise of comfort in later life (that who knows if we'll reach anyway). It just didn't seem healthy devoting the rest of my life to other people's asperities, trials, and turmoil. Plus, I'd made remarkable headway toward my goal and could still eke out a decent chunk of change.

So with the help of Covid, I concluded that it could be worth a portion of the end money to unshackle myself earlier than planned. And I might lasso in a decade or two of freedom (even though landlording truly had become easier for me by then).

I was only sixty-nine when Covid struck in March 2020, and had never planned to sell *that* early. But there must've been some planetary alignment or something …because I'd be seventy in four months and finally receiving Social Security. Plus, by owning a massage business, I qualified for Covid assistance.

But what really forced my hand was that, in Hawai'i during the pandemic—because tourism, almost everyone's source of income, had altogether ceased—ALL tenants were apprised that they no longer needed to pay their rent, but could simply "owe" it.

Wha-a-a-a??

Most bizarre ruling ever!

Meanwhile, (mercenary) landlords—as if they had no financial obligations—were simply hung out to dry, left to somehow collect that rent money "at some later date." Yeah, right.

In August of 2020, my front-unit tenants, a Mexican family, were half planning to vacate September 1st. With one daughter off in college now, they didn't need as much space. But in that crazy Covid climate, they couldn't quite nail down their next move…. The reasonable rent at my place was a bargain, the house was close to their food truck, and I had let them keep the puppy.

But I'd kept them too long (mainly because every time the lease was ending, they begged to stay). Over time, they'd lied about substantial matters—saying they had three kids when they had four, swearing they didn't have a dog when they did, and claiming they only had two trucks when they had three. Yet they never 'fessed up when busted, just stuck to the lies, even in the presence of their children.

"Whose truck is that?" I popped the question one day, after a strange pickup had been parked at the house for two months.

"Oh, y'know, a friend of ours."

Sleuthing at the DMV, I discovered the truck was registered to an unknown man with *their* last name, at *their* address. That's how I learned about both the additional vehicle and the additional child, an older son, returned from the Mainland.

I didn't dislike them; we had a decent rapport most of the time. And the man loved animals and was personable and kindhearted. But the wife was a storm cloud I really lacked the patience for. With Covid in full swing though, their food truck wasn't making enough money. So they started playing footsie about the rent, as *legally* they now could.

"You have to understand," I said, "that even though you're not required to pay the rent during Covid, you're still going to *owe it* to me. So even if you slide for a while, you're gonna end up with debt and that will be stressful for all of us. Better you just pay on time." Plus it was the last month of their lease and they knew I wouldn't renew if they weren't paid up.

Because I needed them to pay that rent, I let them believe I might renew, though I'd firmly decided not to, due to her demeanor, his lies, and the roach infestations in the kitchen and bathroom.

A week late, they paid half their August rent, and asked for an extension on the rest. Hoping they'd come through, I gave them two more weeks to pay the balance. These were, after all, the insane Covid days.

But their next check bounced.

"I won't want to renew your lease," I warned, "if you're not up to date with the rent. I'll give you another five days, but you'll have to pay cash."

Thankfully, they paid it! And then, the very last minute, some relatives offered them a cheaper rental nearby, so they did vacate September 1st. But chasing that rent money throughout August showed me that Hawaiian landlords were getting roasted during Covid. And going forward, the only way I could count on actually collecting monthly rent checks would be through month-to-month leases—since tenants wouldn't get renewed each month if they hadn't paid. And I'd have their security deposit to cover unpaid rent.

But constant turnover would be stressful—an endless string of quirky personas, continuous lease writing, and ever more wear and tear to floors, jambs, and porch railings. Too, month-to-month would mean living on the edge of my seat, because any moment I could receive forty-five days' notice that my tenants were vacating.

Also, remember, *courts don't help you collect money owed you.* There's NO legal route for actually *getting* back rent from tenants. You can go to their bank and establish a lien by showing papers proving you won in court, but if there's no money there....

The Mexicans left me a phenomenal workload in that front unit. But since Covid kept me from doing massage, I had time. And the couple in back, also planning to vacate soon, continued paying their rent so they could count on me as a reference.

So, though still emotionally attached, thoughts of putting the house on the market trickled in. Not only did no one know how long Covid would last, but it happened to be a peak sellers' market. Real estate prices on Kaua'i were higher than ever, with Boomers turning seventy and interest rates unthinkably low. And I knew now that up markets can turn on a dime and another down cycle could be on its way. The 2007 one lasted seven years! So instead of re-renting the front unit, I began fixing it up.

And while sanding floors and painting rooms with my diehard helper, Lila, I gradually and somewhat organically arrived at the conclusion that this wasn't just a good time to sell, but the perfect time. My 1965 house had a new roof, a new exterior paint job, and that adorable new front porch with my pineapple motif. Never again would the place be turned out to this degree. With each passing day, I became more convinced that this was the last time I'd be motivated to perform big repairs and upgrades. Plus I just couldn't bear watching the glory fade all over again with more tenant wear and tear.

True, selling early would mean never living on the fumes of a paid-off house with renters throwing monthly checks at me…. But I'd be free! And would still come away with enough profit to get to my eighties or even nineties. And I had my other house (that was actually paid off) to sell later on, if need be.

The couple in back had never done anything wrong. They too had a dog, as well as Jack, their twenty-four-year-old cat—the young man's *lifelong* companion and older than his girlfriend. They appreciated the back unit since it was off the street and safe for Jack, partially blind. But reaching twenty-five, he'd passed on, and the couple now had more options for living spaces. Also, I'd alerted them I might sell. So when their lease expired in November, they gave notice.

And that helped make up my mind. I listed the house for sale.

With everything in peak condition and no tenants at all, the adjoining inside door was open and the trade winds billowed through. I'd always loved the space as one big four-bedroom/two-bath home surrounded by tropical flowers and fruit-bearing trees. Practically worshipping it now, and hoping some buyer would feel the same, I floated around the tranquil rooms and inhaled that rare access to both front and back yards.

Between final coats of varnish on the new floor, I pinned on an optimistic price—fifty grand more than I was secretly willing to accept. "I'll only part with it for a good price," I told Renee, my new realtor. "I'm a little flexible, but very little. If it doesn't sell, I'll just keep it." She needed to believe a high price was critical to me, because any elasticity I hinted at would be shared with every realtor on Kaua'i—including buyers' realtors—since they're all friends.

Expectedly, Renee pushed back about "comps," comparable properties for sale in the neighborhood, that were priced lower. But my back wasn't against the wall—I didn't need the money, and I wasn't leaving the island. So I didn't waver. "Those comps may have the same number of bedrooms and same square footage," I replied, "but they all have gnarly aspects my house doesn't. My house is beautiful. Besides, comps don't matter to me because my selling price is what the house is worth *to me*. I've owned it sixteen years, lived in it four times, I know all the neighbors, I know what's gone into the renovations."

Deep down though, nostalgia notwithstanding, I was ready to let it go. It was time to move on. Renee, however, didn't need to know that.

"I'm not worried," I said lightly. "Someone will see it for what it is, and that's who I'm waiting for." Though not fully convinced of that, it felt good saying it; selling the house cheap would hurt too much. It was plastered with my blood, sweat, and tears, a ton of all three. In fact, the whole rental property experience was one of the two greatest endurance trials of my life. And the other, "Expedition Costa Rica," lasted six weeks not sixteen years.

Knowing the importance of relationships in her business, Renee stayed cool and didn't press me on the price.

Christmas crept in, both units were empty, and all was quiet. Rent-wise, I could afford to eat it for a few months, but that's never a landlord's preference. And despite the luxury of having the house empty, clean, and showable, it was appearing this sale might take a while…. One low-ball offer came in, but served merely as an annoyance. So I lowered the price by ten grand.

I then found a couple on Craigslist who were so desperate for a reasonable three-bedroom rental that they were offering four months' rent in advance. And rent money up front could be the perfect solution to the Covid protocol, so I met with them.

Middle-aged, no kids, and only one car…they loved the house and wanted it. But, with it being for sale, I explained they'd have to accommodate occasional viewings and even a few open-house sessions. For their cooperation, I offered a modest discount and also said I'd nudge the eventual buyer to keep them on as tenants.

So we signed a six-month lease and they handed me a mountain of cash that was an instant refund for the repairs I'd just completed!

Next I found a short-term renter for the back. Alex, from Massachusetts, just needed a landing place for a few months, so he and I agreed to a six-month lease, that permitted him to leave earlier should he choose.

Greenbacks were flowing in again and I now had the most congenial tenants to date, all fluid with the situation. Both units were kept tidy and spotless, and showings were easy. Renee and I also were mellow as we fielded a couple more unexciting offers.

But another six weeks made it clear my price was still high, so I came down another $12,000. At least I'd tested the market. *LESSON :* Especially if you have good tenants in your units, if you're able to wait, test a high price when first listing your property. Otherwise, if it sells in one week, you'll always suspect you sold too low. It's worth waiting a while for possibly thousands more in profit.

Then one morning around 9:30, my front tenant, Kate, phoned in a panic. "Wendy, there's a man outside cutting down all your trees!!"

"What?!"

"I'm so sorry! I didn't realize what was happening in time to stop him. We were still in bed, and I thought the noise was a lawnmower next door. Then when I finally got up and looked out the window, the guy had cut down all the trees in front!"

"What?! *Who is the guy?* And which trees did he cut?"

"All the trees along the road, except one. I stopped him from cutting the last one. I don't know who he is. But I ran out and screamed for him to stop. Then I asked what the hell he was doing, and he said 'The owner of the house called me and hired me to cut down all these trees.'"

"*What?!*"

"He said some guy called him from his ad in the Yellow Pages and said he'd just bought the house and wanted all the trees in the front cut down."

"Oh my God…."

"He's still here, I stopped him. And I told him that the owner is a woman not a man and that she'd never want those trees cut down."

"I'll be right over. Tell the guy to stay there."

Arriving in tears nine minutes later, I tried to process this nightmarish event. Four out of five of the gorgeous flowering trees I'd planted, practically on day one of owning the house, lay felled across the lawn, while a young man with a chain saw stood by in a mild state of shock.

He verified what Kate had relayed, that some unknown man, claiming to have just purchased the house, had answered his ad and asked what he'd charge to cut down five trees.

"Did he pay you?" I asked the guy.

"He asked me how I get paid, and I told him I could collect the money after I did the job. So he said to text him when I was done."

"Don't you think you should've gotten a little more information about how he was going to pay you, and who he was? For a job like this? Didn't you ask him who was living there and what you should say to whoever was in the house?"

"No, I didn't…. He said just go over and do it."

"You didn't feel he should be there? You were okay just walking onto an unfamiliar property, with cars parked out front, and cutting down all the trees?!" I wasn't blaming the kid, just flabbergasted.

But to make it worse, this twenty-five-year-old guy, clearly inexperienced in just about everything, had zero info to help us find the perpetrator. Having recently arrived from the Mainland, he'd bought himself a chainsaw, placed an ad, and was making fast money. His wife and infant were actually waiting in his parked truck twenty feet away, while he stole a half hour from their beach day to fell my trees and haul them to the dump, in exchange for a few hundred bucks.

As my cherished trees, nurtured from saplings for sixteen years, lay dead across the lawn, their trunks cut to the quick, I had the police come over so I could report the crime. I told the young guy I wouldn't press charges against him. Though in hindsight, I should've held his feet to the fire so he'd help me get to the bottom of what had happened. But I let him off, and he was more than relieved to never look back (and get to the beach). The phone number he gave us for the instigator turned out to be a burner phone or Mainland number that no one answered…so we never got close to identifying who ordered the assault.

And Kaua'i police and detectives are notoriously lame. (Through landlording, I've had enough experience with both to witness how disengaged they are. Even on *Dateline,* they say if you want to get away with murder, Kaua'i's the place.)

My property now looked bare and different…. The whole sardonic event was beyond belief. And all I could do was shake my head.

For about two weeks.

No one (including the "detective" assigned to my case, who I badgerd to no avail) ever even tried to determine who the culprit was. But clearly, I'd been personally targeted.

It wasn't until I told my gardener about it, that I got some insight. "It was probably a previous tenant," he said. "Was there someone who left on bad terms?"

I wracked my brain for which of my rental property tenants would ever commit a hate crime like that. "No, no one." Our issues had never been that severe.

"It could've been someone from farther back than you'd expect," said the gardener. "You know the saying, 'revenge is a dish best served cold.'" I got the chills. I'd never understood that saying until this moment.

Yet it took several more months to realize the tree-cutting had Harvey's signature all over it: calculated cruelty born of a malicious mind, too idle. That's when I realized he was the grapefruit thief, too.

At least he probably felt he'd evened the score now. After that, he appeared to have moved on to his next victim.

Renee and I got a few more nibbles…. Then a pilot showed up. And since the house was eight minutes from the airport (yet no plane noise at the property since the flight path went out over the ocean), and this pilot was on call to fly the emergency rescue plane from Kaua'i to O'ahu, I got excited.

But he didn't make an offer.

No worries though, each passing month of paying down the mortgage meant more profit whenever I did finally sell. My dad had now left this planet, so I was no longer commuting to Long Island; my massage business was thriving; I was writing and publishing books; I was selling my lemons, ~~grapefruits~~, and mangos; I was receiving Social Security; and soon I might have reward money for all my landlord years.

Then the pilot returned and made an offer.

And another buyer showed up simultaneously, so I had two offers, both just under my "secret" acceptable price.

The pilot then upped his bid by $14,000. Knowing how well the property would work for him, I wanted this guy.

And he bought the house.

So it was five months from first listing to closing escrow, but I got someone I felt good about. And he retained the front couple, as I recommended (and who live there to this day), and moved into the back himself, freeing Alex to go live with his girlfriend.

La-de-da, almost a storybook ending. And I strolled away with hundreds of thousands of dollars to leverage a secure financial future, as was the plan. I got $11,000 more than my hoped-for price, and even Renee was surprised.

I wasn't. It was a great house.

≣ *26* ≣

What I Did Right

Though this is a story about learning from mistakes, I shouldn't omit that I actually did a few things right! :)

1. Once I had tenants, I always kept the plants groomed and blooming. And I regularly showed up and scrubbed the common areas like the laundry or garage, often leaving a fresh bar of soap or new scrubby by their outside sink. And with new leases, I always made sure all the lightbulbs were in and working, as well as supplying new sponges, bar soap, a new shower curtain (a shower liner is fine), and an extra roll of toilet paper for their move-in. These friendly gestures were effortless and underscored the c-word.

2. Even with my resentment about testy men at 7 a.m., I discovered that I actually have a decent instinct for renovation and remodeling. Committing to good quality and aesthetics may not have been the popular or thrifty route, but the results a) made me happy, b) made tenants happy, and c) lent confidence that I could sell the house for a good price.

3. I was always fair, never chintzy with workers. No matter how many monetary back flips were happening behind the scenes, my workers weren't privy to my insecurity, gnashing of teeth, or wincing in pain. They received their checks on time and in full every Friday. And the checks never bounced.

Also, I rarely troubled myself with suspicions. I had enough on my plate without being petty, doubtful, or accusative. If a guy was trustworthy and performing well, he was given some leeway. After all, he was doing backbreaking labor all day and all week.

4. I stuck to my guns when I felt strongly about something.

From my downtown New York loft days living in "raw space," as we called it back then, I knew the value of opening up rooms. I'd even once, alone with a hammer and chisel, torn down a double brick wall in a New York Soho apartment to build an arched doorway. So at my rental property, I knew instantly that the small kitchen had to be opened to combine with the living room, and an attractive counter installed where the wall had been. But where I expected workers to chime in with know-how and suggestions, they simply shrugged and questioned how I intended to do it. The know-nothing newbie had to come up with the plan? Yup. All I got from the guys was, "Why are you doing something you don't need to?"

"I do need to, the property needs it."

And, in taking that wall down and even in framing out the empty space where it had been, I had to, blow-by-blow, call all the shots.

I then poked around the granite store and chanced upon a remnant green slab of the exact dimensions needed for my counter. I left one side of it jagged, for charm (the granite guy sanded the sharpness), then had Johnny build slim wooden shelving for supports under each end, with the granite inlaid on top. *LESSON :* When you feel strongly about doing something or doing something a certain way, go for it.

Not only was my new room expansive and light, but that arched opening with the rough-edged granite counter—the horrible idea everyone wrinkled their noses over—was stunning. Nary a soul ever entered the front door again who didn't run their hands over that gorgeous counter and coo with delight. *LESSON :* Every time you push through against the odds, and get what you expected or better, it makes you stronger.

5. Something else I did right (suggested by Vern, the electrician) was having tenants pay for their utilities, gardener fee, and trash collection *with* their rent check each month. And I explained to tenants that, this way, they'd never have to deal with utility bills and their lives would be easier and cheaper.

So, all my landlord years, the utility bills stayed in my name. And I just provided each unit a monthly estimate, based on number of residents, whether they were home all day or at work, whether they were outdoor enthusiasts or sofa spuds, and whether or not they identified as energy-savers. "You have total control over your utility costs," I'd assure them. "I'm not telling you how to live. You can turn off lights and unplug devices you're not using, or leave fans on 24/7. But use less, pay less. Also, since we only have one bill for two units, you'll only have to pay half the service charge." On leases, I'd write, "Monthly utility fees are estimates and may be adjusted if usage is greater or lesser than estimated."

It worked brilliantly. I just kept an eye on the bills to see we stayed in the ballpark. But we never had to change the names on utility bills, and tenants almost never questioned my estimates. At Vern's suggestion, too, my estimates were a smidge higher than the usage guesstimates, allowing me a tiny margin, so if usage was higher for a month or two—like in summer when fans were on—I could let it slide.

6. By maintaining a credit score in the 800 range, I was constantly offered no-interest credit card loans letting me transfer portions of debt into 0% loans for a year or even longer.

7. Moving to Paradise. Though 2600 miles from friends and 5500 miles from relatives, I got to live the dream. The majesty of my surroundings, and Rosie as my adventure buddy, are what made landlording and paying down the debt possible. No matter how tough my job got, the rest of my life was *amazing*. And if the world went to hell in a hand-basket (which it did), I could grow food year round and catch rain water from the sky.

That's why I never got depressed or regretful, and never gave up.

8. Though it was a long and gritty chapter, for the first time in my life, if I could keep my head screwed on, I had a long-term *plan*. And believing my investment solid, I

committed in a way I never had before. Up ahead, if I retained hope, I sensed a distant light that had never been there before. Should my debts continue going down and my real estate up, one day I could sell the rental and "live out my days."

9. And I had other income. There was abundant work massaging tourists, keeping my cash flow stable during lulls between tenants. And with other therapists working for me, I kept my business strong even during extended stays on the Mainland.

10. I put every single expenditure on mileage credit cards (religiously paying the cards off monthly), and earned so much mileage during the remodel and ever thereafter that I never had to pay for flights. And visiting friends and family on the Mainland cleared my head.

I now haven't paid for a plane ticket in over twenty-five years and don't intend to again.

11. My writing was always a creative outlet. About eight years into landlording, I started publishing my books, and being an author gave me both income and an escape from the myopic world of tenants.

12. Getting cooperative tenants into both units while the house was for sale eased the pressure to sell. *LESSON :* Try not to have financial pressure while your house is for sale, so you can both test the market with a higher price and hold out for a higher profit.

Final Lesson and Summary

Congratulations to my dedicated pupils who've stayed to the end of the course! May you thrive and prosper! May you suffer little.

Here are a few final lessons:

Whenever you're motivated to do an exciting upgrade to a house, other than necessities like painting walls and installing new vanities, and especially something you feel in your heart will really compliment the property and make everybody weak in the knees, it's SO worthwhile!

At first it's daunting even thinking about it, because of the cost. And usually it doesn't *need* to be done, hence it's unsettling surging forth on a sketchy vision, often viewed by others as whimsical, risky, or extravagant. But trust your instincts, you won't regret it. I mean, don't go into hock or divorce proceedings, but making a property better is the true joy and FUN of real estate. So, as you're shelling out those thousands, remember everyone who lives there is going to enjoy and benefit from the results for years to come. (Especially projects you've been thinking about for ages.) And these improvements often substantially increase property values.

For many, many years, I was so snowed by responsibility that the pay-off wasn't even on the blip-screen—I never even *imagined* rewards actually materializing. But approaching seventy, I became more aware of how fortunate I'd been for this opportunity to avoid later angst and financial strife.

Yet it still came as a surprise when one day I sensed *for real* that the long-term prospects of my plan were becoming tangible, and I might just make it out the other side. Could it be the worst was behind me? It seemed unfathomable that my debt (my significant other) had become greatly diminished…and that I'd learned the landlord ropes…and that I actually had *confidence* about it all now (and needn't fear the future).

And I was still upright in the saddle. In fact, I wasn't even the same person.

Because I dared to step onto that tightrope, today I'm able to foot the bill for whatever life I choose.

I'd even go as far as saying I'm looking for another dare! Not as crunchy as that last one, please, nor as long-term, but I'd entertain a juicy new opportunity that holds promise. *It's a good thing.* Because when you invest that kind of sweat equity and time, assorted rewards likely WILL materialize. And along with them, satisfaction. And pride that gives you chills.

Sometimes it's just *time*—time to leave a lover, time to move, time to quit a job, time to lose the weight, time to end a friendship, time to speak your truth, time to forgive, time to come clean with yourself about something, or…time to sell a house. I love reaching plateaus.

I view my Landlady in Paradise years as a job well done. Though my plan didn't go as expected—in many ways it went way worse—that's probably just the cost of admission into The Unknown!

But all *did* come to fruition, ending nicely and even ahead of schedule. And where once stood an eyesore, now sits a sweet home. To all who pass, that house suggests what's possible in that little neighborhood. And amongst my few life accomplishments, I can add the restoration of two old plantation houses on the Island of Kaua'i—upgrading neighborhoods and preserving the history of the Aloha State, a true Paradise I love and call home.

I sincerely hope this saga, with all its nail banging and head banging, guides you in either taking on a similar project with more confidence, or avoiding one! At the very least, should you choose the scenic route and go tropical, this tale can assist with some uncertainties about what to expect.

But I must reiterate a final time, that having now shared in all my trials and errors, YOU are far less apt to encounter the hurdles I did. You know now how to approach this kooky profession…one that can masquerade as "just earning passive income." With all my heart—and it's why I wrote this book— I hope this 'How Not To" manual makes your landlord or landlady path easier, more comfortable, and less bumpy than mine. May it spare you the grief new landlords or landladies in Paradise may stumble into when unprepared. You can do it!

Let me know how it goes!

= *END* =

P. S. Just to tie it all in a bow, guess which two people in my story both divorced their spouses, then met on line and married each other.... (!)

Just guess.

I know it's a stretch to picture *any* of these people being a match for each other. But I'll give you two hints: 1) Dave is not one of them. 2) Trisha is not one of them.

But you'll never guess, so I'll tell ya....

Remember Renee, my realtor for the sale? One of the more grounded characters in this book. And remember Rich, the new arrival from Alaska, who, in two shakes bailed to O'ahu with his then-wife and hated me for keeping his deposit when he broke the lease? Well...Renee and Rich are now happily married!

And LOL, you can bet my name came up more than once when they first met. (Pretty sure Rich still resents me.)

But we all wish the happy couple true aloha and all Paradise has to offer!

AFTERWORD

Summary of all Lessons

- In deciding to relocate to Paradise, consider how far you'll be from your parents, and how soon they will be old, and/or how far you'll be from your grandchildren and how soon they'll be older.
- Landlords do best in couples.
- Understand the nature of "long-term," because you may be in this for years or decades.
- Buy in a decent or up-and-coming neighborhood. And the property must have redeeming qualities.
- Factor in the demographics of the neighborhood you're buying into.
- Check the local laws before you buy! In Hawai'i, it's the law that all landlords must live on the island where their rental property is situated.
- It's generally advised that one's rental property be within an hour's drive of one's residence.
- Understand your risk. Even if your property seems an excellent financial bet, your trajectory won't be a predictable graph.
- With a long-term real estate investment, you've got to bargain for recessions, interest rate changes, market slumps, pandemics (!), and natural disasters, not to mention personal or family drama and your own life progressions.
- Landlording is not for everyone.
- Don't hire an inspector referred by your realtor. Anyone working for Team Realtor will likely withhold legitimate concerns, even hideous truths from you.

• It's permissible for a buyer to participate in the inspection. I highly recommend being present for it.

• If you're super hands-on, or want your own creative stamp on the project, you'll have to either be the general contractor yourself or find one who doesn't mind communicating with you and implementing your wishes.

• If you're doing a renovation, try to have a truck or easy access to one.

• Tell construction workers, before hiring them, this is who I am, this is what we're doing here, this is what I expect from you.

• Communicate these "house rules" to new guys coming on the job: "Do it once and do it right" and "We work clean."

• Be clear about what you're asking workers to do, especially if you won't be overseeing the action. It's worth stating, "What I don't want is to pay you to do it, pay you to undo it, then pay you to redo it."

• With construction workers, you need to run a tight ship, but not too tight. You have to find a balance.

• Never pay in advance for work not yet completed.

• Don't expect construction workers to ever give you a break money-wise or time-wise.

• Don't keep workers around who continue bothering you in one way or another.

• There's always another guy out there who can do a job and wants work.

• Require from workers legitimate invoices, printed legibly, and containing all the data needed for your records.

• A tactic some construction workers pull is to fudge their assignment when you're off the job-site. Then when you return and see the work was done differently than you requested, the worker gets additional pay for his time re-doing it.

- Make lists itemizing what you want workers to do.
- Male construction workers may really bristle when you a) suggest different approaches to what they're doing, or b) do anything but praise them.
- Don't think construction guys know how to do all things. Most actually have fairly limited specialties.
- Sometimes you will be the one required to come up with the solution. But it's a confidence builder.
- When you feel strongly about doing something or about doing it in a particular way, go for it.
- Have on hand: a ladder, step-ladder, drop cloths, rags, old towels, newspapers, buckets, soap, sponges, toilet paper, and basic tools like a screwdriver, hammer, tape measure, exacto knife, level, painters' tape, a Sharpie, and solvents like Ajax, Goo Gone, and WD40.
- Although workers have their own tools, keep your own handy—to use or loan—along with generic supplies like a roll of paper floor covering, sandpaper, nails and screws, paper towels, and some cheap paintbrushes.
- Write your name, in paint or indelible ink, on all your own tools and equipment.
- Keeping water or electricity meters in your own name may lead to a little extra money in your pocket.
- Your Landlord or Landlady in Paradise plan may likely work! Investment property is one of the most sure-fire investments out there.
- Hard work pays off. You have the joy and satisfaction of knowing you DID it.

• Have or make a utility closet or shed at the rental property for supplies and tools you'll regularly need there.

• Don't initially be put off by the shabby look of a paint can or even the paint inside it. It might be usable.

• TEST paint colors beforehand, interior and exterior. It's worth the extra time and money. Paint is weird. Even whites are deceptive!

• Mark leftover paint cans as boldly and concisely as possible. I use blue painters' tape and a Sharpie.

• Or preserve your mental health and heaps of time and use only off-white paint.

• Get all the free advice you can when tradesmen come to give estimates. Interview several for a cross-section of opinions.

• Interview construction workers long enough to get a good take on them. If they're flirting, late, changing the appointment time at the last minute, too rushed, smell like beer, or have their baby in the truck…beware.

• Get a P.O. box for your address on any and all correspondence with tenants, including the lease. Tenants should not know where you live.

• Convey to all tenants that this lease, these pages we're signing, are for real. "Read them carefully, abide by them, and we'll be fine."

• For many landlords, especially those with multiple properties, using a management company is a no-brainer.

• Different sized units attract and accommodate different family configurations. A three-bedroom will likely attract families with children, a one-bedroom will draw singles or couples.

• Tenant problems cannot become your problems, or your goose is cooked.

• You'll never get a complete handle on dealing with tenants. So don't expect to master that part of the job. Focus on a cool mindset instead.

• Don't take tenant issues personally. Just go by the book.

• Discriminate! Screen the heck out of your applicants. Screening is how you save yourself time, energy, and headaches.

• Never rent to anyone based on a ten-minute walk-through and a filled-out application. An in-depth interview is critical. When they get chatty, much is disclosed.

• Try hard to meet everyone who will be in the household, including children and dogs.

• The "security deposit" is so named because it's a landlord's only stash to clean, fix things tenants break, or cover any rent they may owe upon departure.

• A full security deposit should be collected with every new lease and all the guidelines pertaining to it honored.

• Make sure you have that security deposit money on hand at refund time!

• It's not your job to take the moral high ground. Your job is to maintain the property, collect the rent, and keep decent people in your place.

• Tenants can and will break leases. And it's really not illegal.

• You don't want renters building stuff, storing stuff, or planting stuff. No fence, no shed, no vegetable garden, no fruit trees.

• You don't want tenants to have leverage. That's why you don't have them over for pizza. Give them a centimeter, they'll take an acre.

• Alcohol is a landlord's worst enemy.

• Should you be sharing the same property with tenants, you may want to initially offer lower rent to draw in a higher number of applicants to choose from.

• Never go to war with your tenants. Never confront them with aggression or anger. Landlords can't "pick their battles," because landlords can't *have* battles.

• You need a good lease. Other landlords or realtors or property managers can probably steer you to a good one.

• You need a pro-landlord lease.

• References from mothers and other relations are worthless.

• Keep personal control over the yard.

• In certain economic downturns, you may need to lower the rent but, unless your place is a dump, don't drop it so low you attract bottom feeders.

• You may feel compromised rejecting certain people, but if you go soft and "try to help them," you're making a mistake.

• Keep extra sets of doorknobs, and learn how to change them out.

• "Wear and tear" happens—scuff marks on baseboards and dings in doorjambs, thresholds, and wood floors—from furniture being moved in and out.

• Doorjambs must be safeguarded because they can't be replaced (without extreme complication and expense). And they're jeopardized every time tenants move in or out.

• A paper trail is mandatory should you find yourself in court. Anything without proof holds zero weight with a judge.

• In any written letter, clarify that you're addressing everyone living there. Name each one.

• You can't have too much in writing, so be prepared to write letters now and then.

• Renting to unmarried couples can be risky.

• If you need tenants and aren't getting enough bites, lower the rent price.

• People haggling over every dime will probably continue haggling over *every* dime.

• Never be desperate! And never make important decisions out of desperation.

• "Sleep on it" whenever there's even the smallest doubt regarding important decisions.

• Don't make assumptions. Especially about potential tenants.

• Tough experiences may leave scars.

• Finances aren't the only thing to derail a landlord. Tenant drama, drugs, lies, and uncertainty can cause more grief than a bounced check.

• If tenants are taking pictures of "issues" or potential issues at your property, they may be collecting "exhibits" to show the judge.

• Never be a no-show in a court case; you automatically LOSE by default!

• If landlord claims, in writing, that tenant owes landlord more than the security deposit (that tenant wants returned), then tenant might not sue landlord for that deposit since landlord can countersue tenant for an even higher amount.

• If no one is holding a valid lease, no one can deny that the landlord has the right to live there now.

• Let tenants know in advance, and write in the lease, that they'll receive their deposit or balance due within two weeks after they vacate.

• Keep sufficient cash on hand to cover the weeks or even months when a unit may sit empty as you hold out for desirable tenants.

• If you have time to wait, and especially if you have tenants in your units, test a high price when you first list your property for sale. Because if it sells in one week, you'll always suspect you sold too low.

• Try not to have financial pressure while your house is for sale, so you can both test the market with a high price and also hold out for a good price.

• Stick to your guns. Every time you push through against the odds, and get what you expected or better, it makes you stronger and builds confidence.

• Tenacity can really pay off. Long-term rewards CAN be reaped.

Use this QR code to
buy my books and ebooks
with one click!

Use this QR code to read reviews
of my books with one click!

OTHER BOOKS BY AUTHOR

I Did Inhale – Memoir of a Hippie Chick
Stars in Our Eyes – 20 true stories
Some Swamis are Fat
Expedition Costa Rica *
Nicaragua Story – Back Roads of the
Contra War
Silence of Islands – poems
Ta Ta for Now – the movie

– all in paperback and ebook –
(audio soon)
Available wherever books are sold or loaned
If not in your book store or library,
just request them.

'Expedition Costa Rica' might be a good
next choice for intrepid types like you.

Thanks for reading <u>Landlady in Paradise</u>.
If you enjoyed it,
please put a review on Amazon!

And visit: <u>WendyRaebeck.com</u>